THE NEW TESTAMENT AND
ITS TRANSMISSION

THE BAIRD LECTURES FOR 1929-30

Reproduced by kind permission of 'The Times.'

Two Leaves of a Papyrus Codex of the Second or Third Century showing Rom. XI. 24-32 and Phil. IV. 14-23 with Col. I. I.

From the Chester Beatty Collection. See p. 192.

THE NEW TESTAMENT
AND ITS TRANSMISSION

BY

GEORGE MILLIGAN

D.D. (ABERDEEN), D.C.L. (DURHAM)

PROFESSOR OF DIVINITY AND BIBLICAL CRITICISM IN THE
UNIVERSITY OF GLASGOW

With a frontispiece and six facsimiles

HODDER AND STOUGHTON
LIMITED   LONDON

FIRST PRINTED IN 1932

PRINTED IN GREAT BRITAIN BY ROBERT MACLEHOSE AND CO. LTD.
THE UNIVERSITY PRESS, GLASGOW

TO THE
PRINCIPAL AND SENATE
OF THE
UNIVERSITY OF GLASGOW

FOREWORD

THE FOLLOWING lectures were delivered in 1930 under the Baird Foundation, and I gladly take this opportunity of thanking the Trustees for the honour they did me in appointing me to the Lectureship and for their kind co-operation in the discharge of its duties.

The lectures were originally delivered from notes with the aid of lantern illustrations, and I have not thought it necessary to remove any traces of their colloquial character. The whole contents have, however, been thoroughly revised and extended, and in the latter connexion I have not hesitated to draw from earlier writings of my own on the same and kindred subjects.

I desire also to emphasize that I have had in view throughout not the professional student for whom there is ample material available, but the ordinary Bible reader who is conscious that much work has been done in recent years in the textual criticism of the New Testament, and is anxious to be assured that its writings have come down to him as nearly as possible in the words of its first writers. For the convenience of such readers, Greek and Latin terms are rarely used except with their English equivalents, and a short Glossary of technical terms has been added ; while the Additional Notes and Selected Bibliography point to the means for further study of the questions raised.

It remains only to express grateful acknowledgment to Messrs. Hodder & Stoughton for undertaking the publication of the Lectures, and to the readers and compositors of the Glasgow University Press for the excellence of their work.

G. MILLIGAN.

The University,
 Glasgow,
 August, 1932.

CONTENTS

LECTURE III

THE ANCIENT VERSIONS

LECTURE IV

CRITICAL EDITIONS OF THE GREEK NEW TESTAMENT

LECTURE V

THE EARLY ENGLISH VERSIONS

LECTURE VI
THE AUTHORISED AND REVISED VERSIONS

APPENDIXES

CONTENTS

LIST OF PLATES

[Most of the facsimiles have been reduced in size, in order that complete pages may be shown.]

LECTURE I

THE ORIGINAL WRITINGS OF THE NEW TESTAMENT

' For me the archives are Jesus Christ : the inviolable archives are His Cross and Death, and His Resurrection and the faith that is through Him ' (IGNATIUS, to the Philadelphians, viii.).

THE ORIGINAL WRITINGS OF THE NEW TESTAMENT

' We have this treasure in earthen vessels, that the exceeding greatness of the power may be of God, and not from ourselves ' (2 Cor. iv. 7, R.V.).

Introductory.

THE NEW TESTAMENT contains for us the best wisdom in the world, and no effort can be too great to learn all we can regarding its contents and the manner in which they have come down to us.

It is with the latter enquiry that we are specially concerned in the present course of lectures.

All know how easy it is to forget that the New Testament has a history of eighteen hundred years behind it, and that during that period, unless the text had been miraculously preserved, which would have been contrary to God's ordinary mode of dealing, it was subject to all the dangers attending the transmission of any book, however precious, during a long period of years. And the more so, when we remember that during three-fourths of that period it was subject to the further danger of transmission by copies made by hand. We cannot wonder then that the question has often been raised : What security have we that the original text has been preserved in all essential particulars ?

Or, look at it in this way. What of the mass of variant readings of which we hear so much, and for whose existence we have only to point to our Revised Version ? No one can compare that Version with the Authorised Version without recognizing that in a large number of cases the Revisers must have had a different Greek text before them, and that, to judge from such marginal notes as ' Some ancient authorities read . . . ,' ' Some ancient authorities omit . . . ,' and ' The two oldest Greek manuscripts, and some other authorities, omit . . . ,' they themselves were often at a loss as to which reading should be preferred.

Of course, if the original writings had survived, there would have been no difficulty in answering these and similar questions. But they have long since perished, either in the ordinary course of tear and wear, or in the destruction of sacred writings which accompanied persecution in the Early Church, and we must look to other measures for confirming our New Testament text.

PLATE I.

FRAGMENTS FROM A PAPYRUS ROLL OF LATE THIRD CENTURY,
CONTAINING ST. JOHN XV. 25—XVI. 2 AND XVI. 21-31.

Discovered at Oxyrhynchus (Oxyrh. Pap. x. 1228), and gifted by the
Egypt Exploration Society to Glasgow University Library. See p. 5.

And here it is that the science of Textual Criticism comes in : for the main function of that discipline is to carry us back behind the vast number of variant readings which have arisen in the history of the New Testament to the exact words of the original writers, so far as these can now be recovered. And here let me say that while it is not possible in the present enquiry to discuss at any length the principles underlying this science, the science itself is based on well-defined rules of procedure and is not the haphazard process which some people are apt to imagine it to be. We shall meet with many illustrations of this from time to time in our enquiry. Meanwhile, let me direct attention to one or two particulars regarding the New Testament as a whole, which have a closer bearing upon its history and transmission than may perhaps at first sight appear.

External Form.

To begin then with the *external form* of the New Testament writings. We know that the books of the Old Testament were written on vellum, but there can be little doubt that the books of the New Testament were written on papyrus rolls in accordance with the general practice of the time. These rolls were so named because they were formed from the papyrus plant. The pith of the plant was cut into narrow strips, which were laid down vertically to form a lower or outer layer. Over this a second layer was then placed, the strips this time running horizontally, and then the two layers were pressed together to form a web or sheet. A single sheet was, as a rule, 5 to $5\frac{1}{2}$ inches in width and 9 to 11 inches in height, but when more space was required this was easily obtained by fastening a number of sheets together. A roll of twenty sheets, which could be divided at will, was, apparently, a common size for selling purposes. The price naturally depended on the quality of the papyrus, but it cannot have been a cheap substance, and, indeed, was often dearer than the vellum in ordinary use.

The writing was arranged in columns of from two to three inches wide and was, as a rule, confined to the side on which the fibres lay horizontally, technically known as the *Recto*, but it could be extended to the *Verso*, or back, if necessary. A good example is afforded by Rev. v. 1 where, by his reference to ' a book written within and on the back,' the seer evidently wishes us to understand that so great was the number of woes to be recorded that the *Recto* of no ordinary roll could contain them, and that both sides of the papyrus had to be employed (cf. Ezek. ii. 10).

Used sheets were often turned to different purposes, their first contents having been crossed or washed out (cf. Col. ii. 14), as when we find a private letter written over the effaced notice of a death, or as when the *Verso* of an old taxing-list serves the schoolmaster and his pupil for a writing lesson.

Character of Script.

The *script* in the case of the New Testament writings would doubtless be a careful non-literary hand, which would vary according to the education and skill of the writer. There were no breaks between the words, the letters being run on continuously, so that it is difficult at times to know where one word stops and the next begins. What is implied may be seen by printing a few words of our English New Testament in this way :

INTHEBEGINNINGWASTHEWORDANDTHE
WORDWASWITHGODANDTHEWORDWASGOD

Considerable difficulty must, in consequence, have been caused to copyists, especially if the letters could be divided up in different ways, as when, to use a familiar illustration, ' NOWHERE '

may represent ' NOW HERE ' or ' NOWHERE.'
Abbreviations in the way of leaving out the last
syllables of familiar words were frequent and, as
a rule, accents and breathings were only spar-
ingly employed. The bearing of these facts
upon the various readings that crept later into
our New Testament texts is at once obvious.

As showing the approximate size of the New
Testament autographs, it has been calculated
that a short Epistle, like the 2nd Epistle to the
Thessalonians, would be a roll of about 15
inches in length with the contents arranged in
some five columns, while St. Paul's longest
Epistle, the Epistle to the Romans, would run
to about 11 feet and a half. As regards the
Gospels, St. Mark would occupy about 19 feet,
and St. Luke about 31 or 32 feet, while the Revelation of St. John might be estimated at 15 feet.[1]

Addressing of Rolls.

It remains only to notice that the manuscript when completed was rolled up, much as
we roll up a map, and fastened loosely with a
string, without going through the formal process of sealing, which was customary in the case
of more official documents. The *address* of the

[1] See F. G. Kenyon, *Handbook to the Textual Criticism
of the New Testament* (London, 1912), p. 34.

Church or person for whom it was intended was added on the outside, and, if we may judge from the general practice of the time, that address was stated in the briefest possible form. No more was needed, seeing that the roll was entrusted for delivery to a passing friend or traveller to whom the address was known, and who would be personally acquainted with any further details required. At the same time, owing to this very brevity of address, many questions which have exercised scholars have arisen. For example : Who were the Galatians to whom St. Paul wrote ? Were they the inhabitants of a district in the north of Asia Minor or of a Roman Province visited by St. Paul on his first and second missionary journeys ? Or again, Is the destination of the Epistle to the Hebrews to be found in Jerusalem, or in Alexandria or in Rome ?

The roll form determined the manner in which its contents were read. Holding the roll in his left hand, the reader gradually unrolled it with his right, rolling up again with his left hand what he had already read. The fact that the roll was not divided into chapters or verses would make quotation very difficult, and, consequently, scribes were apt to trust more to their memories than was consistent with strict accuracy.

Use of Dictation.

Another feature of the New Testament on which fresh light has been thrown is the use of *dictation* by some, at any rate, of its writers. We are apt to think of dictation as a purely modern convenience, but evidence is multiplying as to the large use made of it by all classes of writers from a very early date. Nothing is more common, for example, than to find at the close of a papyrus document such words as ' I, A, on behalf of B, seeing that he was unable to write for himself,' and though an educated man like Paul had no need to have recourse to such an expedient, we may be sure that he would gladly avail himself of the assistance of a pupil or friend in the actual writing of his Epistles. Thus, in Rom. xvi. 22, ' I Tertius, who write the epistle, salute you in the Lord,' we find Tertius definitely claiming to be the writer of the Epistle, and in that capacity sending his own closing greetings along with those of others. And when in 2 Thess. iii. 17 the Apostle adds his authenticating signature, ' The salutation of me Paul with mine own hand, which is the token in every epistle : so I write,' the natural conclusion is that the body of the Epistle was written by someone else (cf. 1 Cor. xvi. 21 ; Col. iv. 18). Gal. vi. 11, ' See with how large letters I have written unto you with mine own hand,' is particularly interesting in this respect, for here we find Paul reminding his converts that contrary to his usual practice he had written to them with his own hand. Why? Was it not because of the severity of the Epistle's contents? With his wonted forbearance and tact the Apostle did not wish that any scribe should come between him and those he was obliged to rebuke in such strong terms, the ' large ' letters of which he made use lending further emphasis to what he wrote.

Shorthand.

Along with the use of dictation, the question may be raised, though it cannot be definitely answered, as to the possible use of *shorthand*. Some form of shortened writing was undoubtedly current at the time, and we can now supplement the evidence regarding its use by an interesting papyrus letter from Oxyrhynchus of the year A.D. 155.[1] In it, an ex-magistrate apprentices his slave to a shorthand writer for two years. The teacher is to be paid 120 drachmae, of which sum he has already received a first instalment of 40 drachmae. The second instalment is not to be paid until the boy has

[1] *Oxyrhynchus Papyri* iv, p. 204 f., No. 724.

learned the whole system, and the third only
when he ' writes fluently in every respect and
reads faultlessly.' In view of this and similar
examples, it would not, then, have been astonishing if certain New Testament scribes had
recourse to some such system, but, as has
already been stated, this is mere conjecture and
may seem to be hardly in keeping with the art-
less character of the first Christian documents.

Epistolary Form.

Keeping still to points of external contact
between our New Testament writings and the
general practice of the time, it is interesting to
notice that the Epistles or Letters, which form
the largest proportion of the books of the New
Testament, are couched in the common *epistolary form* of the time. They begin with an
address such as ' A to B, heartiest greetings.'
This is followed by a prayer for those to whom
the letter is addressed, and this again by a
thanksgiving for what measure of good fortune
has befallen them. Then come the special
contents of the letter, the whole ending with
greetings and a valediction. Address, Prayer,
Thanksgiving, Special Contents, Personal Salu-
tations, and Autographic Conclusion—this with
the customary variations is the ordinary form

of a papyrus letter, and by his adoption of it Paul imparted a directly personal note to what are too often exclusively regarded as theological treatises or religious essays.[1]

When, then, we think of Paul at work on one of his letters, we can imagine him pacing up and down the room, his thoughts fixed on some distant Church and, as its needs rose up before him, pouring forth his glowing sentences to the scribe sitting at his feet. And when the scribe's work is done, revising what he has written and adding his authenticating signature ' with my own hand Paul ' to show that in reality the whole letter comes from him. It would be interesting to know how much Paul left to his scribes. As a rule, he doubtless dictated word for word, but may it not be that in some cases he left a certain amount of freedom to his scribes, which helps us to explain the differences of language and style which have perplexed scholars ?

Language.

Nothing has as yet been said of the *language* of the New Testament.

In view of the fact that all its writers, with the probable exception of Luke, were Jews, we

[1] See Additional Note A.—Greek Papyrus Letters.

might naturally have expected that Hebrew or
Aramaic would be made use of as in the Old
Testament writings, but as a matter of fact
recourse was had, in almost every instance, to
Greek. Nor is the reason far to seek. At the
beginning of the Christian era Greek was in
general use throughout the Roman Empire,
much as Latin reigned supreme during the
Middle Ages, or French in the eighteenth century. It had penetrated even to Palestine, and
along with Aramaic was employed by all classes
of the population. The relation of the two languages comes out clearly in the striking scene
depicted in Acts xxi. 37 ff., where it is obvious
that the Jerusalem mob whom Paul addressed
from the stairs leading up to Antonia expected
that he would have addressed them in Greek,
and that it was his falling back on their native
Hebrew or Aramaic that led to their being ' the
more quiet.' [1]

It must be kept in view, however, that this
Greek was not the Greek of the great Attic

[1] An interesting parallel may be quoted from a bilingual
district of Ireland, where, at a public discussion between a
Protestant and a Roman Catholic champion, any approach
to a disturbance was at once quelled by a few words in
Irish. ' The people were listening to English speeches,
but the Irish touched their hearts more nearly.' See T. K.
Abbott, *Essays chiefly on the Original Texts of the Old and
New Testaments* (London, 1891), p. 164.

writers, but a more common and vernacular language, which was understood and made use of by the great mass of the people. With the bearing of this fact upon the interpretation of the New Testament vocabulary we are not at present directly concerned, but we may note in passing that it led later copyists to improve on what they regarded as the ' vulgarisms ' or ' colloquialisms ' of the original texts.

Before we leave the external form of our New Testament writings, it may be well to recall two changes which took place at an early date in their history.

Papyrus Codices.

The first of these was the substitution of *papyrus codices* for papyrus rolls. The word ' codex ' meant originally the trunk of a tree, then a block of wood split up into leaves or tablets (cf. Luke i. 63 ; Isai. viii. 1, xxx. 8), and then a book or writing whose leaves were not rolled within one another like the papyrus rolls of which we have been thinking, but were laid over one another like the leaves of a book. It is obvious that such a form had many advantages, rendering possible, for example, the use of both sides of the leaf and the consequent gathering of the separate writings into one volume. It was a form, at any rate, which particularly commended itself to Christian writers from the third century onwards, judging from the number of examples of it which recent discovery has brought to light. One well-known instance is afforded by the leaf of a papyrus book, containing a considerable portion of the first chapter of Matthew, which can claim to be a fragment of one of the oldest manuscripts of any part of the New Testament in existence. It was, again, on the leaf of a papyrus codex that, in 1897, Dr. Grenfell and Dr. Hunt detected what purport to be certain new Sayings of Jesus, and, most recently of all, a papyrus codex going back to the third century has been brought to light, which contained when complete not only all four Gospels, but the book of Acts as well.[1]

Parchment.

But there was a further change of still greater moment in the material employed for our New Testament texts when papyrus gave place to *parchment*. Papyrus, though very durable, is, at best, a brittle substance, lending itself readily to *lacunae* or breaks, and a great step forward

[1] See Additional Note B.—Recent Archaeological Discoveries.

was taken towards the preservation of the original text by the adoption of the more durable parchment or vellum, prepared from the skins of calves or other animals. In a rough form parchment was in use before papyrus as a writing material, but towards the close of the second century B.C. a finer substance was produced for literary purposes, and this came to be employed for the great New Testament copies of the fourth century onwards.

Here we may notice the double or even triple use to which sheets of vellum were sometimes put. When scribes were at a loss for a fresh sheet, they not infrequently scraped out the original contents and superimposed new contents. The document then came to be known as a *palimpsest*, literally ' written over again.' In the circumstances the earlier writing was often the more valuable of the two, and, as we shall find, cases are not wanting of rich additions to our Biblical texts coming from some such unexpected sources.

Multiplication of Copies.

In ways such as these, then, we must picture to ourselves the original writings of the New Testament—a number of separate papyrus rolls, or later, of papyrus or parchment codices of various sizes, written for the most part in colloquial Greek, and circulating only amongst the readers to whom they were in the first instance addressed. But, as time passed, the need of additional copies made itself felt. The Church, which was the happy possessor of one Apostolic epistle or letter, would be encouraged to add others to its collection (cf. Col. iv. 16), while individual believers would also wish copies for themselves. The result was the rapid multiplication of copies of our New Testament books, and, as these copies were made by hand, it was inevitable that they would be exposed to all the dangers attending such a process.

We shall see directly what some of these dangers were. But before we do so it may be well to emphasize two considerations of a general character.

The first was that early copies would be made by the writer's pupils or friends, and that consequently the same degree of accuracy could not be looked for as in the case of the work of professional scribes.

The second was that the New Testament texts were not from the first invested with the same sanctity as were the Old Testament Scriptures, and that at times the scribes would be content if they gave the general sense of a passage without being too particular as to the exact wording.

Rise of Variant Readings.

Keeping, then, these considerations in view, we have now to ask what was the nature of the *variant readings* of which we have been speaking. They have been classified in different ways, but may be conveniently summed up under the two heads :

(1) Unintentional,
(2) Intentional,

although it is not always easy to distinguish between the two.

As regards the *unintentional* variants, we have to reckon with mere slips of the pen which even the most careful copyists find it difficult to avoid. There is again the substitution of one synonymous word for another, or the insertion of a connecting word or proper name for the sake of clearness, as when ' Jesus ' takes the place of the indefinite ' He ' in such a passage as John vi. 14 ; or, once more, the frequent changes of order in familiar words or phrases as when ' Jesus Christ ' is substituted for ' Christ Jesus ' or *vice versa*.

Of a more serious character is what is techni-

cally known as *homoioteleuton*, or the confusion
of words or phrases of like ending. Let me
cite a description of what is meant. ' Suppose
. . . that a transcriber is copying a passage in
which the word " disciples " is read at the end
of two successive verses. He transcribes the
first verse, and then, looking up from his work
to the copy before him, his eye unfortunately
lights upon the end of the second verse, no
part of which has yet been written. He sees
the word " disciples " which his pen has just
traced ; and, not perceiving that the second
verse in which it occurs still remains untran-
scribed, he proceeds with his work, and leaves
out that verse altogether. . . . For an example
we may refer to Matt. xii. 47. That verse is
entirely omitted in some excellent manuscripts.
And, for a very obvious reason. It ends in the
Greek with exactly the same word as the pre-
ceding verse (λαλῆσαι, " to speak "), and has
thus, in some cases, been altogether overlooked
by transcribers.' [1]

With this there may be compared what is
known as *dittography*, or the writing of the
same word twice when it should only be written
once.

---

[1] See *The Words of the New Testament as altered by
Transmission and ascertained by Modern Criticism*, by W.
Milligan and Alex. Roberts (Edinburgh, 1873), p. 15.

The *intentional* mistakes are equally varied. Thus, as we have already seen (p. 15), there is a tendency on the part of copyists to correct the language and style of the original documents, in the interests, so they imagined, of the documents themselves. And a somewhat similar tendency led to the practice of introducing harmonizing words or phrases, as when the words ' to repentance ' are added by the later scribes in Matt. ix. 13 and Mark ii. 17, in order to conform with the text of Luke v. 32, ' I came not to call the righteous, but sinners to repentance.'

Additions to the original text are also common, in many cases arising from the inclusion of words or phrases in the text which first of all had found a place in the margin. Thus, if you consult a Revised Version you will find that the words in John v. 4, ' For an angel went down at a certain season into the pool, and troubled the water : whosoever then first after the troubling of the water stepped in, was made whole of whatsoever disease he had,' are omitted by many ancient authorities and are probably to be regarded as an explanatory gloss which was taken over from a marginal note into the regular text. And along with this may be mentioned the paragraph John vii. 53-viii. 11 —the story of the woman taken in adultery—

which, while undoubtedly embodying a true tradition, does not belong to the original text of St. John's Gospel, but was placed there for purposes of preservation. And so again, the Doxology attached to the Lord's Prayer in Matt. vi. 13, ' For thine is the kingdom, and the power, and the glory, for ever. Amen,' is wanting in our best Greek manuscripts, and was doubtless added at a later date on liturgical grounds to convey the people's response to the Prayer.

Greater difficulty is caused by dogmatic changes, though it may be questioned whether these are really as numerous as is sometimes made out. Two may be noted. One is Acts xx. 28, where many ancient authorities read ' to feed the Church of the Lord ' (not of ' God ') in view of the words that follow ' which He hath purchased with His own blood ' ; the other is 1 Tim. iii. 16, where, in the supposed interest of the Divinity of our Lord, ' God ' takes the place of ' He who.'

It is not necessary to go on quoting. Let any reader just think of the different kinds of mistakes into which he would most readily fall when copying a document of any considerable length, and he will understand the dangers which beset the New Testament scribes. So far, too, from these dangers being of late growth,

as was at one time thought, they make their
appearance from a very early date.

Number of Variants.

As to the actual *number of variants* in the
early ages of the Church, we have naturally no
exact data, but in John Mill's Greek Testament
published in 1707, of which we shall hear
again (see p. 107), the variants have been
estimated at 30,000, and this number has been
enormously increased in recent years, perhaps
to 150,000 or even more. It is not to be
wondered at that the mere mention of such
figures has caused deep anxiety in many minds,
and has led to the belief that the New Testament text is in a very corrupt state. But we
must keep steadily in view that the great mass
of these variants are of a very trivial character
and in no way affect the general sense, and
further, that if the variants are many, the means
for judging amongst them are exceptionally
numerous and convincing. So numerous and
convincing that, according to our great English
critics, Bishop Westcott and Professor Hort,
' if comparative trivialities, such as changes of
order, the insertion or omission of the article
with proper names, and the like, are set aside,
the words in our opinion still subject to doubt

can hardly amount to more than a thousandth part of the whole New Testament.' [1]

Need of Enquiry.

Why then, someone may say, concern ourselves about the matter at all ?   The answer surely is easy.   In the case of an ordinary book this or that reading may not matter much.   But in the case of the New Testament, with its far-reaching and authoritative claims, no effort can be too great to ensure that we possess its message as nearly as possible in the very words of the original writers, recognizing with Origen, the first great Biblical critic, that ' there is not one jot or tittle written in Scripture, which does not work its own work for those who know how to use the form of the words which have been written.'

[1] See *The New Testament in the Original Greek*, small edition, p. 565.

LECTURE II

THE GREEK MANUSCRIPTS

' What manner of things lie in your case ? demanded the Proconsul of a North African Christian Speratus about the year A.D. 180. " Books," was the answer, " and Epistles of Paul a just man." '

THE GREEK MANUSCRIPTS

'The cloke that I left at Troas with Carpus, bring when thou comest, and the books, especially the parchments' (2 Tim. iv. 13).

Summary.

IT IS with the New Testament and the manner in which it has come down to us during the eighteen hundred years of its history that we are concerned, and in my last lecture I carried you back to the beginning of that history and tried to give you a general idea of the outward appearance of our New Testament autographs when they left their first writers' hands. They were written, as we saw, in Greek, on papyrus rolls, and were at first circulated separately ; but, as time passed and copies were multiplied, these took the form of papyrus or parchment codices, instead of papyrus rolls, and a beginning was made of collecting the New Testament writings into small groups, and afterwards into a single volume.

An obvious result of this multiplication of copies was the rise of a large and ever-increasing number of variant readings, and the main object of our present enquiry, let me once more emphasize, is to get behind these variants, and to recover, as far as possible, the words of the original writers.

Materials for Restoration of Text.

The materials at our disposal for this purpose are generally reckoned as three in number : (1) **Greek Manuscripts,** or copies made by hand of the New Testament writings or of parts of them ; (2) **Ancient Versions,** or translations of the Greek New Testament into other languages such as Syriac or Latin, and (3) **Patristic Quotations,** showing how the passages cited by early Christian writers were read.

Papyrus Texts.

Clearly, for our purpose, the Greek Manuscripts are the most important, and of these the earliest are a few *papyrus texts*, the recovery of which is one of the romances of recent New Testament Archaeology. We cannot tell the story now. It must be enough that in digging for papyri in Egypt the explorers unearthed a certain number of leaves containing portions of the New Testament. Upwards of forty of these fragments have been deciphered and edited, some containing a text which must go back to the second century. With the exception of a roll containing one-third of the Epistle to the Hebrews, they are all of a very fragmentary character, and their main interest consists in their early date and in their relation to the various readings which are found in the great parchment manuscripts of the fourth and subsequent centuries.

Parchment Manuscripts.

These parchment manuscripts fall into two groups : *uncials* and *cursives* (or *majuscules* and *minuscules*) according to the mode of script. Thus, the word uncial, which is doubtfully derived from the Latin *uncialis*, ' inch-long,' is used of a style of writing in which each letter is separate and of a rounded or capital form, as distinguished from cursive writing, or writing in a running hand with the letters joined together. In the older text-books the eighth or the ninth century was regarded as the dividing line between these two modes of script, but there is now abundant evidence that cursive writing was used from a much earlier date for non-literary purposes, and it is better, therefore, to use the word cursive as a general term of all writing in a running hand whatever the date, and to adopt minuscule for the literary or Biblical cursive.

As regards their numbers, the uncial manuscripts may be reckoned at about one hundred and seventy, of which, however, only fifty are really of consequence, while the minuscule manuscripts may be reckoned at two thousand three hundred, and their number is constantly increasing.

For convenience the uncial manuscripts have been distinguished since 1751 (see p. 110) by the capital letters of the alphabet—Codex A, Codex B, and so forth, while the minuscule manuscripts are denoted by numbers—1, 2, 3, and so forth. Obviously it will be necessary to limit ourselves to a few of the most important manuscripts, and in doing so we begin naturally with the Codex Vaticanus or Codex B, which is generally held to be the most valuable of all our manuscripts of the New Testament.

Codex Vaticanus (B).

The *Vatican manuscript*, as its name suggests, is preserved in the Library of the Vatican in Rome, and, though its early history is wrapped in great obscurity, we know that it has been catalogued in that Library at least since 1475.

For long, great difficulties were placed in the way of its inspection, and it was not until it had been carried off by the Emperor Napoleon in 1807 to Paris that it was examined and its value recognized by the Roman Catholic scholar Hug.

In 1815 the Codex was restored to the Vatican, and in 1843 the German critic Tischendorf inspected it for two days of three hours each. Two years later an English scholar, Tregelles, was allowed to look at it, but his pockets were first searched, his writing materials taken away, and two clerics stood behind him ready to snatch away the volume if he looked too long at any passage.

In 1857 a very faulty edition was issued by Cardinal Mai. Other editions followed, including an edition of the New Testament in 1868, prepared by Vercellone and Cozza. But all editions are now supplanted by the splendid phototype copy published by Hoepli (Milan) in 1904 under the auspices of Pope Pius X. The colour of the parchment, the ink, and all the details of the writing are faithfully reproduced, so that scholars have now an exact facsimile in their hands.

As regards the original manuscript, it is written on fine vellum made from antelopes' skins with three narrow columns of 42 to 44 lines each to the page, while the writing resembles that of the best literary papyri of the first and second centuries, small, simple, but beautiful uncials, without stops or accents or divisions. Originally the manuscript contained the whole Greek Bible, with the exception of the books of Maccabees, but, as regards the New Testament, the latter part of Hebrews (from chap. ix. 14), the Catholic Epistles and the Apocalypse have been lost.

The order of the books in the New Testament varies in certain particulars from that to which we are accustomed. The Gospels and Acts come first, but the Catholic Epistles are inserted between the Acts and the Pauline Epistles, and Hebrews precedes the Pastorals.

Various copyists have been at work on the manuscript, and in the tenth century the original writing was traced over by a scribe who feared that the precious letters might fade and be lost. However much we may regret the excess of zeal in this particular case, it is only fair to take the opportunity of paying a warm tribute to the care and toil of these early scribes, and to the devotion, in the highest sense of the word, which characterized their work—a devotion fittingly recalled by the words which Longfellow puts into the mouth of Friar Pacificus in the *Golden Legend* :

I come again to the name of the Lord !
Ere I that awful name record
That is spoken so lightly among men,
Let me pause awhile and wash my pen ;
Pure from blemish and blot must it be
When it writes that word of mystery !

. . . .

Yes, I might almost say of the Lord,
Here is a copy of thy word
Written out with much toil and pain ;
Take it, O Lord, and let it be
As something I have done for thee.

The place of origin of Codex Vaticanus has
been widely discussed, but it is now generally
assigned to Egypt, while its date falls in the
second quarter of the fourth century, representing a second or third century text. The early
date is thus a strong argument for its general
correctness, though the errors which have been
detected forcibly remind us that the evidence
of even the best codex cannot be regarded as of
paramount authority.

The interesting conjecture that Codex Vaticanus and its ally Codex Sinaiticus, of which we
shall hear directly, form two of the fifty copies
of the Bible prepared by Eusebius at the order
of the Emperor Constantine for the churches in
his new capital of Constantinople, is no longer
supported by critics ; but great weight is

attached to the agreement of the two manuscripts in the case of contested readings, and it
is generally acknowledged that, along with the
Codex Sinaiticus, the Codex Vaticanus presents
' the simplest, shortest, and concisest text.' [1]

Codex Sinaiticus (א).

Our next codex, the *Codex Sinaiticus*, recalls
one of the most striking discoveries in recent
years in connexion with Biblical texts.

In the year 1844 Tischendorf, on the occasion of a visit to the monastery of St. Catherine
on Mount Sinai, noticed in the library a basket
with a large number of stray leaves of manuscripts, amongst which were several leaves of
the oldest Greek writing he had ever seen. Of
these leaves he extracted forty-three, containing
parts of the Greek Old Testament, and was
casually informed by the librarian that two
similar basketfuls had already been used to light
the monastery fires. Tischendorf was permitted
to keep the forty-three leaves, and published
them in 1846 under the name of the *Codex
Friderico-Augustanus* as a gift to King Frederic
Augustus of Saxony.

In 1853 he revisited the monastery in the

[1] See P. Schaff, *A Companion to the Greek Testament and
the English Version* (London, 1883), p. 119.

hope of further discoveries, but could learn nothing of the manuscript, and on the occasion of a third visit in 1859 it seemed as if he were to fare no better, until one evening shortly before his departure the steward of the monastery put into his hands a number of loose leaves wrapped in a red cloth. Judge of Tischendorf's amazement and delight when he discovered that these were the very leaves of which he was in search. He was allowed to keep them in his room all night, ' and that night it seemed sacrilege to sleep ' (*quippe dormire nefas videbatur*). ' There by myself,' he tells us, ' I gave way to my transports of joy. I knew that I held in my hand one of the most precious biblical treasures in existence.' With the aid of Tsar Alexander II, the Patron of the Greek Church, Tischendorf had the manuscript sent after him to study, first at Cairo and then in Russia, and after being exhibited in various places it was sent in 1862 to St. Petersburg, to find a resting-place in what was then the Imperial Library, in return for various gifts to the monks at Mount Sinai. The symbol א, the first letter of the Hebrew alphabet, was assigned to the Codex as all the English capital letters were already taken up. We may add that a facsimile edition of the Codex was issued by Tischendorf in 1862 from type specially cut to imitate the letters of the manuscript ; but even this great achievement is now superseded by the facsimile photographed by Helen and Kirsopp Lake in 1911, to which Professor Lake has prepared an Introduction, summarizing all that can be learned of the history of the Codex.

Like the Vatican Codex, the Sinaitic Codex was once a complete Greek Bible, but, unlike it, it has still the New Testament complete—*the only uncial manuscript of the New Testament of which this can be said*—along with the first known copy in Greek of the Epistle of Barnabas and a portion of the Shepherd of Hermas—an interesting testimony to the place which these writings held in the mind of the early Church.

The Codex was written on fine vellum, with four narrow columns to the page, and there is again strong evidence that it was written in Egypt, and not, as is sometimes held, in Rome or Caesarea. Many correctors have been at work on the original text, which must go back to the fourth century, though somewhat later than the date of the Codex Vaticanus. Its value is, therefore, again everywhere admitted, and, as has already been stated, along with the Codex Vaticanus, it is our principal authority for the reconstruction of the critical text of which we are in search.

PLATE II.

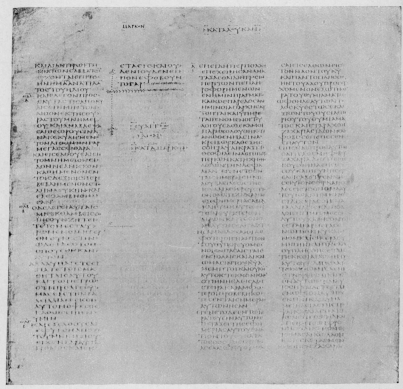

From Sir Frederick Kenyon's 'Handbook to the Textual Criticism of the New Testament,' by kind permission of Macmillan & Co. Ltd.

CODEX SINAITICUS, FOURTH CENTURY.

The page shown contains Mark xvi. 2—Luke i. 18, the last twelve verses of Mark being omitted. See p. 37.

A clear example of the agreement of the two codices is afforded by the closing verses of St. Mark's Gospel. Both manuscripts break off suddenly with the words of verse 9 ' for they were afraid ' (ἐφοβοῦντο γάρ), and in both cases leave the rest of the columns blank as if the scribes looked forward to supplying an ending from some other source.

It is impossible to enter here on a discussion of the critical questions involved, but in view of the combined authority of the two great manuscripts, even when the mass of other manuscripts is against them, there is widespread agreement amongst scholars that the real ending of St. Mark's Gospel has been lost (as the last portion of a papyrus roll, it would be easily detachable from the rest), and that the ending we now have was added at a later date to complete the narrative.[1]

The same two manuscripts are again agreed in omitting ' first-born ' (πρωτότοκον) in Matt. i. 25, and in Luke ii. 14, both, along with other authorities, support the reading which has aroused so much criticism : ' Glory to God in the highest, And on earth peace among men in whom He is well pleased '—a reading which differs from the Authorised Version only by a

[1] See further Milligan, *New Testament Documents*, pp. 274 ff.

single letter in the original Greek (εὐδοκίας
(gen.) for εὐδοκία (nom.)). On the other hand,
in Luke xxii. 43 f., the Codex Sinaiticus along
with most uncials includes the incident of the
bloody sweat as against Codex Vaticanus which
omits it, and, in Luke xxiii. 34, it, with most
uncials, has the words ' Father, forgive them for
they know not what they do ' against Codex
Vaticanus. Or to take one other example of the
independence of the two codices, while Mark,
according to the Vatican Codex, heads his
Gospel ' The beginning of the Gospel of Jesus
Christ, the Son of God ' (i. 1), the Sinaitic
Codex omits the words ' the Son of God.'

Codex Alexandrinus (A).

From the Codex Sinaiticus, the ' pearl of all
his researches,' as Tischendorf calls it, we pass
to a codex which is of very special interest to us,
as it forms one of the principal treasures of the
British Museum. It is known as *Codex Alexandrinus*, or Codex A, and was originally copied
in Egypt, whence it was taken by the patriarch
Cyril Lucar to Constantinople. In 1624 he
offered it to King James I, and on James's
death the gift was transferred to Charles I in
1627. At a later period the manuscript had a
narrow escape from destruction when fire broke

out at Abingdon House, Westminster, where the King's Library was then lodged, and an eye-witness has drawn a vivid picture of its custodian, the great classical scholar Richard Bentley, hurrying out of the burning library in his nightgown and his great wig, clutching the precious manuscript under his arm.

When the Royal Library was presented by George II to the nation in 1753, the manuscript found its present home in the British Museum, where it is publicly shown at the end of the King's Gallery.

When complete, the manuscript contained the whole Greek Bible with the Epistles of Clement, while the Psalms of Solomon were also at one time included. From an Arabic inscription on the first sheet it has been thought that the manuscript was written in Egypt by the pen of the martyr Thecla shortly after the Council of Nicaea, but this belief may have arisen from the fact that the manuscript, as we have it now, begins with Matt. xxv. 6, which is the lesson of St. Thecla's Day in the Roman Calendar.

In the Gospels the Codex contains a somewhat late and revised text in substantial accord with the text underlying our present Authorised Version. In the Apocalypse, on the other hand, the text is of an earlier type and is perhaps the best extant manuscript of that book. The letters are written continuously as in our other uncial manuscripts, and the ends of sentences are punctuated by points. In the initial lines of certain books vermilion takes the place of black ink. The manuscript is generally assigned to Egypt, and mainly on palaeographical grounds is dated in the fifth century, probably the first half of the century, but in any case later than the two great codices, the Vatican and the Sinaitic, of which we have been thinking.

The manuscript shows the usual scribal errors, amongst which Scrivener (*Introduction* [2], i. p. 105) draws special attention to the ' portentous ' reading in John xix. 40, where the contracted form for ' God ' ($\theta\bar{v}$) is substituted for the contracted form for ' Jesus ' ($\bar{w}$), making the sentence run, ' So they took the body of God, and bound it in linen cloths with the spices.'

Those who wish to form a clear idea of the manuscript's appearance should consult the edition in reduced photographic facsimile brought out by Sir Frederic G. Kenyon for the Trustees of the British Museum.

It may be noted that the manuscript is the first uncial manuscript to be used by scholars for critical purposes (cf. 107).

Codex Ephraemi Rescriptus (C).

We have traced the history of our three great Greek Bibles, the Vatican, the Sinaitic and the Alexandrine, which are distributed amongst the three capital cities, Rome, Leningrad and London, and are the treasured possessions of three branches of the Christian Church, the Church of Rome, the Eastern Church, and the Church of England. And now for our next codex we turn to yet another capital, Paris, as the present home of the *Codex Ephraemi Rescriptus*, literally ' the Codex of Ephraem written over again,' whose cumbrous title introduces us to another of the romantic stories which surround our New Testament text.

In the sixteenth century there was in the possession of Cardinal Ridolfi of Florence a manuscript containing certain tracts of Ephraem the Syrian (died A.D. 372). After various vicissitudes the manuscript passed into the hands of Catherine de' Medici, who carried it with her to Paris. There was no thought of the manuscript being anything else than a transcript of Ephraem's tracts, but one day a careful student detected faint traces of an underlying text. The document was in fact a *palimpsest* (see p. 17), and the original writing when disclosed proved to be considerable portions of a Greek Bible—

fifty-four pages of the Old Testament and one hundred and forty-five of the New. These were deciphered by Tischendorf with his usual skill, and their date fixed in the fifth century. An excellent facsimile page containing Matt. xx. 16-34, and showing the underlying text appearing through the superimposed writing, is provided by Sir Frederic Kenyon in *Our Bible and the Ancient Manuscripts*, p. 139, where he also draws attention to the fact that in verse 16 our Codex is the chief authority for the words ' for many be called, but few chosen,' while in verses 22-23 the words ' and to be baptized with the baptism that I am baptized with ' are added, though they are omitted in the Vatican and Sinaitic manuscripts. In both cases the readings of Codex C may be traced to the habit which scribes have of introducing into the narrative of one Evangelist words and clauses from the corresponding description of the same events in the other Evangelists (cf. p. 21).

Codex Washingtonianus (W).

Amongst the many interesting documents brought to light in Egypt in recent years there have hitherto been comparatively few Biblical texts of importance and these, for the most part, very fragmentary (cf. p. 28 f.). Widespread interest accordingly was aroused some twenty-five years ago when it became known than an exceptionally rich find of Biblical manuscripts had taken place in Egypt, comprising the books of Deuteronomy and Joshua, the Psalms, the Gospels, and fragments of the Pauline Epistles. The Arab dealer who first offered them for sale declared that they had been discovered at Akhmîm, where the copy of the apocryphal Gospel of Peter was found in 1885, but he has since admitted that he did so only to mislead, and the exact locale remains somewhat of a mystery, though a prayer in the subscription to the Gospel of St. Mark is sometimes taken as pointing to the ancient monastery of the Vine-dresser, situated near the Third Pyramid. In some such ruined monastery or tomb, at any rate, the manuscripts must have lain undisturbed for a long period of years, to judge from the desert sand with which their leaves, when first opened, were found to be encrusted.

It is now known that an attempt was made to secure the precious documents for the British Museum, but before this could be carried through they were purchased by a wealthy American, Mr. C. L. Freer, of Detroit, Michigan. In consequence, they were at first described as the Freer Manuscripts, but as Mr. Freer has deposited them in the Smithsonian

Institute at Washington as a gift to the nation the nomenclature now adopted is the *Washington Manuscript*, or, more shortly, Codex W. Meanwhile, with great generosity, Mr. Freer is doing everything in his power to make the contents as widely available as possible. The work of editing has been entrusted to the skilled hands of Professor Sanders of Michigan University, who, in addition to a beautiful facsimile edition of the Four Gospels, has issued a monograph on *The Washington Manuscript of the Four Gospels* (New York, Macmillan Company, 1912), from which the following particulars are mainly drawn.

The Codex contains the Gospels in the order Matthew, John, Luke and Mark, and even in antiquity seems to have been an object of peculiar sanctity. Professor Sanders gives a curious proof which may not be altogether convincing to everyone. On the first page of each Gospel there are several large blots. Small bits of these blots were ' cleared off,' and on analysis were found to be formed of vegetable or animal matter. And Professor Sanders thinks we may ' safely assume ' that they came from the dripping of candles or lamps, probably the former to judge from their thickness. As a flock of wool was found between two leaves—evidently used as a book-mark—sheep were probably kept in the neighbourhood of the monastery, and the inference that the candles used were of tallow is easy. The blots cannot have come from any natural use in reading, as then they would have been found in other parts of the manuscript. ' It seems that this Bible must have been kept in some dark part of the monastery and, when shown to visitors, usually only the first pages of Matthew and John were looked at, but the more curious or distinguished visitors may have been shown the first page of each gospel.'

The contents include, as has already been stated, a practically complete text of the four Gospels, the only leaves wanting being those which contained John xiv. 25, xvi. 7, and Mark xv. 13-38, while it should further be noted that the first quire of John (i. 1 to v. 12) is in a different hand from the rest, and may have been added at a later date. The material employed for the original manuscript is parchment, generally made from sheepskin, and though the leaves have necessarily suffered from age and exposure, the characters can still be read with wonderful ease. Each of the three hundred and seventy-two written pages consists of a single column of thirty lines, differing in this respect from the Vatican and Sinaitic Codices, which show three and four columns to the page respectively, no doubt a reminiscence of the narrow columns of the papyrus rolls from which they were copied. The letters, as is the general rule in all early uncial manuscripts, follow each other closely without any division into words, and there is very little punctuation. On the other hand, distinct phrases are clearly marked off by numerous blank spaces, and paragraphs are distinguished by inserting the first letter of each new paragraph in the margin. To discuss the manuscript further from this point of view would, however, lead us into many technicalities of little interest to the general reader, and it will be better simply to notice the character of its testimony with regard to one or two familiar texts whose reading differs from the text underlying our Authorised Version.

Thus, in Matt. xi. 19 Codex W reads with the Vatican and Sinaitic Codices, ' Wisdom is justified by her works,' instead of, as in the Authorised Version, ' of her children,' and in Mark iii. 29 joins the same authorities in finding the man who blasphemes against the Holy Spirit ' guilty of an eternal sin,' rather than ' in danger of eternal damnation.' In Luke ii. 14 the angels' song of praise appears in the form we have already noticed (cf. p. 37) : ' Glory to God in the highest, and on earth peace among men in whom He is well pleased,' and in chap. xxii. of the same Gospel verses 43-44 which narrate the incident of the bloody sweat in the Garden of Gethsemane are omitted. The mention of the angel of the Lord in connexion with the moving of the water in John v. 4 similarly disappears, and our Codex is again at one with most ancient authorities in showing that the section regarding the woman taken in adultery (John vii. 53 to viii. 11) is no part of the original text of the Fourth Gospel, however true the tradition which it embodies.

As against these omissions, the Washington Manuscript gives one addition to the commonly received text which has evoked much discussion. We have already seen that there are various problems raised by the ending of St. Mark's Gospel, and if we are to follow the weight of evidence, both external and internal, there seems little doubt that the ending to which we are accustomed did not form part of the original Marcan document (cf. p. 37). And now the Washington Codex comes forward with a wholly new passage interpolated immediately after our Mark xvi. 14. The passage runs as follows :

And they excused themselves, saying, This world of iniquity and of unbelief is under Satan, who by reason of unclean spirits suffereth not men to comprehend the true power of God. Therefore reveal thy righteousness now. They said these things to Christ. And Christ answered them : The term of years of the power of Satan is fulfilled, but other dangers are nigh ; and for the sake of them that sinned was I delivered up unto death that they might return unto the truth and might sin no more ; that they might inherit the spiritual and incorruptible glory of righteousness which is in heaven.

Then the narrative is resumed at chap. xvi. 15 as found in our Authorised Version.

That the ending of the Washington Codex cannot be accepted as authentic may be at once admitted ; but the words are at least an interesting survival of tradition from an early age, and help to illustrate the varied and far-reaching character of the questions which surround the history of our Gospel text.

As regards the date of the manuscript, scholars are satisfied, on palaeographical grounds, that it cannot be placed later than the fifth century, and may, in all probability, belong to the fourth.[1] In this way the Washington Codex at once takes its place amongst our earliest authorities for determining the Greek text of our Gospels. It is too soon to say what is its precise value in this direction, but

[1] A subscription in small uncials of the fifth century shows that the manuscript was at that time in the possession of a certain Timothy—' Holy Christ, be thou with thy servant Timothy and all of his.'

Professor Sanders has already made it clear that what New Testament critics know as its ' type ' of text varies considerably in the different parts. Its scribe, or the scribe of its parent (or parents), has obviously been dependent upon distinct manuscripts with differing pedigrees, perhaps because, as Professor Sanders suggests, its origin is to be traced to a time when Biblical manuscripts came near extinction in certain regions owing to the early persecutions of the Church. It may prove on further examination that Professor Sanders' analysis of the ' patch-work ' character of the parent manuscript is over-elaborated. But, in any case, there can be no question that, more particularly in the Gospels of Mark and John, it contains many curious and interesting readings whose true position in the reconstruction of our New Testament text is still under discussion.

Codex Bezae (D).

We come now to what is one of the most curious and interesting of all our New Testament manuscripts, known as *Codex Bezae* (or D). At one time it was in the possession of the reformer, Theodore Beza, who presented it to the University of Cambridge in 1581. He himself is said to have obtained it from the monastery of St. Irenaeus at Lyons when that city was sacked by the Huguenots. Of its earlier history very little is known, but it is possibly the ' very ancient Greek manuscript ' which the Bishop of Clermont produced at the Council of Trent in 1546 in support of the Latin reading in John xxi. 22, ' *Si eum volo sic manere* ' (' *If I wish that he should so remain* '), and we know that some use was made of it by Stephanus in the 1550 edition of his Greek Testament and by Beza himself in his own later editions. Recently, Professor Ropes has made out a strong case for Sicily as its place of origin, and sees no good reason why it may not be assigned to an early date in the fifth century.[1]

The Codex contains most of the Gospels of Matthew, John, Luke and Mark in that order and the Book of Acts, along with a few verses of 3 John. One of its most striking features is that it is bilingual, the Greek and Latin texts facing each other on opposite pages, with the Greek in the place of honour on the left. This would seem to indicate that in the community where it was produced the Bible was generally read in Greek, but that the community itself was Latin-speaking, and that consequently the Latin version - acted, according to Professor Souter, as a ' sort of crib ' to the Greek.

[1] *The Beginnings of Christianity*, Part I. iii., p. lxvii. f.

With the view of further assisting the reader, the scribe has broken up his text into sense-lines of varying lengths, each line conveying a distinct idea. This will be seen more clearly by printing a few lines in a very literal English translation of Acts i. 1 ff. The words in italics appeared in the first draft of the text but were afterwards excised :

The former treatise I made
concerning all things, O Theophilus,
which Jesus began both to do
and to teach, until the day
He was taken up, after He had given com-
    mandment through the Holy Spirit
to the Apostles whom He had chosen, *and
    ordered*
to proclaim the gospel ;
to whom also He showed himself alive
after His passion by many proofs,
for forty days,
being seen of them and speaking
the things regarding the Kingdom of God :
and, being assembled together with them,
He charged them not to depart
from Jerusalem, but to wait
for the promise of the Father,
which ye heard, *saith He, from my mouth* :
for John indeed baptized with water ;
but ye shall be baptized with the Holy Spirit,
and which ye are about to receive
after these not many days
until the Pentecost.

The general character of the text varies largely from the normal type in the way of *additions* and *omissions*, as the following examples show.

Thus, to take *additions* first, in place of Luke vi. 5, which is transposed to follow verse 10, Codex Bezae inserts the following words : ' On the same day, seeing one working on the Sabbath day, He (Jesus) saith unto him, Man, if thou knowest what thou doest, blessed art thou ; but if thou knowest not, thou art accursed and a transgressor of the law.'

And our codex is again the principal authority for the words inserted after Matt. xx. 28 : ' But seek ye to increase from that which is small, and to become less from that which is greater. When you enter into a house and are summoned to dine, sit not down in the highest place, lest perchance a more honourable man than thou shall come in afterwards, and he that bade thee come and say to thee, Go down lower ; and thou shalt be ashamed. But if thou sittest down in the worst place, and one worse than thou come in afterwards, then he that bade thee will say to thee, Go up higher and this shall be advantageous for thee ' (cf. Luke xiv. 8-11).

The *omissions* are even more striking. Thus, in Luke xxii. 19 f. the second mention of the cup in the institution of the Lord's Supper disappears. In Luke xxiv. 40 the familiar words

' And when He had said this, He showed them His hands and His feet ' are no longer read, and the same thing applies to John iv. 9, ' for Jews have no dealings with Samaritans.'

In the Book of Acts alone there are so many variations of text that widespread currency has been given to the view that Luke wrote two editions of Acts, the first a longer one represented by the text of Codex Bezae and the second a shorter one corresponding to the text underlying our Authorised Version. The question must be left to experts, but one or two further examples of interesting readings may be cited. Thus, in Acts xi. 28 an additional clause is added with reference to the visit of the prophets to Antioch to the effect ' *and there was much rejoicing ; and when we were gathered together* one of them named Agabus . . . ,' where the use of the pronoun in the first person suggests that Luke himself was actually present. In chap xii. 10 a local touch is given to the account of Peter's escape from prison by the statement ' they went out, *and went down the seven steps*, and passed on through one street.' According to chap. xix. 9, we are told that Paul was discoursing ' daily in the school of one Tyrannus *from the fifth till the tenth hour* '; while in chap. xix. 28 we read that the craftsmen ' were filled with wrath, *and they ran into the street*, and cried out saying, Great is Diana of the Ephesians.' Of much greater significance is the absence from Acts xv. 20 of the reference to ' what is strangled ' (καὶ πνικτοῦ), implying that we have here a later interpolation, unknown to the earliest texts, and suggesting that the decree does not deal with ceremonial law, but is confined to certain ethical observances—an attitude strikingly emphasized by the further addition of the golden rule in its negative form, ' *and that whatsoever they would not should be done to them ye do not to others.*' [1]

It is impossible to go on quoting, but enough perhaps has been said to justify Sir Frederic Kenyon's description of the Codex as ' the most peculiar, and in some respects the most remarkable, of the Greek MSS. of the New Testament,'[2] and the importance of its readings is emphasized by Professor Hort in the words, ' When every allowance has been made for possible individual licence, the text of D presents a truer image of the form in which the Gospels and Acts were most widely read in the third and probably a great part of the second

[1] The Codex was edited by Scrivener in 1864, and for a popular account of it reference may be made to Canon J. M. Wilson's recent study on *The Acts of the Apostles* (London : S.P.C.K., 1923).

[2] *Handbook*, p. 88.

century than any other extant Greek manuscript.' [1]

Minuscule Manuscripts.

We cannot carry further our account of the
Greek uncial manuscripts,[2] nor can we linger
at any length over the *minuscule* manuscripts.
They belong to the ninth century onwards and
do not, therefore, make the same appeal to us
as do the early uncials. But their very number
(cf. p. 30) makes them impressive, and their
value for textual purposes is being increasingly
recognized. It will be remembered that they
are denoted by the arabic numerals 1, 2, 3, 4,
etc. Let me mention one or two specimens :

Codex 1 : An eleventh century manuscript
now at Basle, which was used by Erasmus
in preparing for the first printed and
published Greek New Testament (cf.
p. 100 f.).

Codex 33 : A ninth century manuscript at
Paris, known as ' the Queen of the
cursives ' on account of the antiquity and
excellence of its text.

Codex 69 : A manuscript of the fifteenth
century preserved at Leicester. It belongs to what is known as the Ferrar

[1] *Introd.*[2], p. 149.
[2] See Additional Note C.—Additional Uncial Manuscripts.

group of manuscripts, which, amongst other peculiarities, insert John vii. 53-viii. 11 after Luke xxi. 38. And

Codex 461 : which is dated A.D. 835, and enjoys the distinction of being the earliest dated Greek manuscript on vellum.

Here, then, we must leave our Greek manuscripts. It has been possible to indicate only certain aspects of them, but apart from the light which they throw on our New Testament text, they are in themselves of absorbing interest. They carry us back in their principal exemplars to an all-important period in the history of the Church, when Christianity came to be recognized as the State Religion and the humble papyrus rolls gave place to the magnificent vellum codices of the fourth and succeeding centuries. They remind us of the countless generations of readers who have gazed upon them and drawn light and guidance from their contents. And they confirm for us the truth of our Lord's own words, ' Heaven and earth shall pass away ; but My words shall not pass away ' (Luke xxi. 33).

LECTURE III

THE ANCIENT VERSIONS

' Therefore blessed be they, and most honoured be their name, that break the ice, and give the onset upon that which helpeth forward to the saving of souls.   Now what can be more available thereto, than to deliver God's book unto God's people in a tongue which they can understand ? '

(The Translators to the Reader, 1611.)

THE ANCIENT VERSIONS

' How hear we, every man in our own language, wherein we were born ? ' (Acts ii. 8).

WE HAVE seen already the widespread use
of Greek even in Palestine at the beginning of
the Christian era, and that in consequence the
books of the New Testament written in that
tongue would be generally understood. Gradually, however, as the missionary activities of
the Church developed, the need of translations
would make itself felt, and was met by the
appearance of versions or translations of our
New Testament in some of the leading languages
of the ancient world. Regarding the evidence
of these versions one thing is clear, that they
are only secondary witnesses, and consequently,
so far as we are at present concerned, are to be
studied not so much for themselves as for the
light they throw on the Greek text underlying
them. It must also be remembered that the
text of these versions as they have come down
to us is often corrupt, and that while some
versions are very literal, others indulge largely

in paraphrase. Notwithstanding all this, however, the versions are of great importance from their early date—going back in some cases to a text of the third or even the second century—from their witness to the readings peculiar to certain districts, and from the light which they throw on the question of additions and omissions in the texts from which they are derived.

Syriac Versions.

Of these early versions, we must again, as in the case of the Greek manuscripts, confine ourselves to a few of the most important, and in doing so it is natural to begin with the Syriac Versions, if only because they are written in a Syriac or Aramaic dialect very closely akin to the Aramaic spoken in Palestine in the time of our Lord and in which He conducted His teaching. In listening to these versions we are, therefore, in a sense listening directly to our Lord Himself, just as we do in the few Aramaic phrases which still remain embedded in our Greek Gospels (Mark v. 41, Ταλειθά κούμ, Mark vii. 34, Ἐφφαθά, Matt. xxvii. 46, Ἐλωΐ ἐλωΐ λεμὰ σαβαχθανεί;).

The first centre of Syriac-speaking Christianity would seem to have been Edessa, east of the Euphrates, and its introduction into this country has been traced to King Abgarus who died in A.D. 50. According to the account preserved by the Church historian Eusebius (*Church History*, i. 13), Abgarus had sent an embassy to Palestine, who on their return journey heard of the fame of Jesus, the Messiah, and reported to Abgarus what they had learned. Abgarus was so much impressed by what he heard that he addressed a letter to Jesus, referring to the miraculous powers attributed to Him, and said that he himself had come to the conclusion that Jesus was either God or the Son of God, and besought His aid in the grievous sickness from which he was suffering, adding that he had ' a very small, but noble city which might be sufficient for them both.' To this letter Jesus is reported to have replied that He must fulfil the things for which He had been sent, and that after He had been received up to God He would send one of His disciples to heal Abgarus and to give life to him and those who were with him.[1]

The story has found support but is doubtless legendary. It is generally agreed, however, that Christianity started at Edessa among the Jews and was first preached there by a Jew, Addai, from Palestine before the middle of the second

[1] For the complete text of the two letters, see Additional Note D.—The Abgarus Letters.

century. This resulted in the rise of Syriac
Versions, and several interesting discoveries
have been made recently in connexion with
them. Three in particular demand our attention.

The Diatessaron.

Eusebius (*Church History*, iv. 29) tells us that
about the year 170, Tatian, an Assyrian Christian, who had studied under Justin Martyr in
Rome, published a Harmony of the Four
Gospels, known as the *Diatessaron*, or the Gospel
' at the hands of four ' (διὰ τεσσάρων), which
was ' still in the hands of some '. The
importance of such a document is obvious, but
no trace of the original, either in Syriac or in
Greek, was forthcoming, and opponents of
Christianity began to express doubts as to
whether it had ever existed. But now with the
aid of a Commentary on the Diatessaron by
Ephraem, a Syrian Father, and certain Arabic
and Latin translations, these doubts have been
refuted, and a reconstruction of the text of
what one of its editors, Mr. Hamlyn Hill, de-
scribes as *The Earliest Life of Christ* has been
published. A page from Mr. Hill's edition in
English will give an idea of its character. The
references on the right side of the page show how
the Four Gospels have been woven into one story.

Then cometh Jesus from Galilee to the Jordan unto John, to be baptized of him. And Jesus was about thirty years of age, and was supposed to be the son of Joseph. Now John saw Jesus coming unto him, and saith, This is the Lamb of God, which taketh away the sin of the world. This is he of whom I said, After me shall come a man, which is preferred before me, for he is before me. And I knew him not; but that he may be made manifest to Israel, for this cause am I come baptizing in water. Now John was forbidding him, saying, I have need to be baptized of thee, and comest thou to me? Jesus answered him, and said, Suffer *it* now: thus it becometh us to fulfil all righteousness. Then he suffered him. And when all the people were baptized, Jesus also was baptized; and he went up straightway from the water: and the heaven was opened unto him. And the Holy Spirit descended upon him in the form of a dove's body: and lo, a voice from heaven, saying, This is my beloved Son, in whom I am well pleased.

Mt. iii. 13

Lu. iii. 23

Jn. i. 29

Jn. i. 30

Jn. i. 31

Mt. iii. 14

Mt. iii. 15

Lu. iii. 21

Mt. iii. 16

Lu. iii. 22

Mt. iii. 17

The Harmony raises many questions regarding the history of our Gospels which cannot be discussed now. What we are mainly concerned with is the witness which it bears to their text at a very early date, and consequently the support it gives to, or withholds from, many important readings in our Greek manuscripts. With the Vatican and Sinaitic Codices, for example, it omits the last twelve verses of Mark, and also agrees with the Vatican Codex in omitting the incident of the bloody sweat (Luke xxii. 43 f.). Other notable readings are Luke ii. 14, ' Glory to God in the highest, and on earth peace, and good hope to men ' ; Matt. xviii. 14, ' Even so your Father, which is in the heavens, willeth not that one of these little ones should perish, whom after erring he calleth to repentance ' ; Mark x. 51, ' What wilt thou that I should do unto thee ? And the blind man said unto him, My lord and master, that thou mayest open mine eyes, and I may see thee ' ; Luke xxiii. 26, ' And Jesus went on with his cross behind him ' ; John xix. 19, ' And Pilate wrote on a tablet the cause of his death, and put it on the word of the cross above his head.'

Such, then, is Tatian's Diatessaron, and its popularity in the early Syriac Church is shown by the fact that for a time it seems to have completely taken the place of the individual Gospels, to judge from the fact that only two copies of the latter have come to light.

The first of these again supplies us with a romantic story.

The Curetonian Syriac Gospels.

In 1838 Archdeacon Tattam visited the library of the Monastery of Saint Mary Deipara in the Natron Valley, west of Cairo, in search of ancient manuscripts. He was cordially welcomed by the monks, and, according to a picturesque account that has reached us, was ' taken to a vaulted room which had neither door nor windows and could be entered only by a trap-door from above. He was lowered down into this cellar, furnished with a candle, and left to make his own investigation of a large mass of manuscripts covering the floor to a depth of one or two feet.' Of these manuscripts some forty eventually found their way to England and were placed in the British Museum under the charge of the Rev. William Cureton, who discovered amongst them a fragmentary manuscript of the Syriac Gospels, now known by his name. The manuscript belongs to the first half of the fifth century, but points back to a much earlier text, which on examination proves to be closely related to the same type of text as in the Diatessaron. Cureton himself claimed that he had discovered a text of Matthew's Gospel practically in the terms which Matthew used. Of the earlier history of the manuscript little or nothing is known, but it is headed. by the strange title ' Evangelion da-Mĕpharrĕshê Mattai,' which is generally understood to mean the Gospel of the ' separated ' one, as distinguished from the harmonized narrative of Tatian. Upon the opening sheet the following note has been inserted in a hand of the tenth century :

This book belonged to the monk Habibai, who presented it to the holy monastery of the Church of the Deipara belonging to the Syrians in the desert of Scete, that God, abounding in mercy and compassion for the sake of whose glorious Name he separated and gave this spiritual treasure, might pardon his faults and forgive his shortcomings and number him among His own elect in the day that His mercy cometh to life, by the prayers of all the circle of the Saints. Amen, amen.

Son of the Living God, have pity in the hour of Thy judgment on the sinner that wrote this. Amen !

The Lewis Syriac Gospels.

For our second Old Syriac Version of the Gospels we are indebted to the twin Cambridge scholars, Mrs. Lewis and Mrs. Gibson, who discovered the codex containing it at the monastery of St. Catherine on Mount Sinai, to which reference has already been made as the home of the Codex Sinaiticus. The monastery is situated in a narrow valley 4,500 feet above the level of the Red Sea, and some 2,800 feet below the summit of Jebel Mousa. From a very early period a community of monks had lived there, and when in the sixth century the monastery was converted into a fortress by Justinian, monks from the surrounding monasteries sought refuge in it along with their treasures. The result was the accumulation of great stores of important manuscripts—Greek, Arabic, Syriac—mostly stored away in chests and very inaccessible. Amongst these, in 1868, Professor Palmer caught a glimpse of ' some curious old Syriac books and one or two palimpsests ' (*Desert of the Exodus*, i. p. 70), and in 1889 Dr. Rendel Harris recovered a Syriac translation of the long-lost *Apology of Aristides*, a defence of Christianity addressed to the Emperor Hadrian.

The conviction thus awakened that there were still further discoveries to be made led Mrs. Lewis and Mrs. Gibson to visit the monastery in 1892. Among the ancient volumes produced for their inspection was a thick volume whose leaves had evidently been unturned for centuries, as they could be separated only by manipulation with the fingers or by the steam of a kettle. The manuscript proved to be a *palimpsest*, the upper writing containing an account of the lives of certain women saints of date A.D. 697, while the underlying and more ancient writing proved to be a copy of the Four Gospels, the pages being headed ' Evangelium ' ' da Mathai,' ' da Marcus ' or ' da Luca.' Mrs. Lewis photographed the whole volume, and on her return to Cambridge submitted the result to Professor Burkitt, who saw that the volume contained a very early text closely akin to the Curetonian text. (See Plate IV.)

A second expedition was then organized for transcribing the text directly from the manuscript, in which Professor Bensly, Professor Burkitt and Dr. Rendel Harris took part. And to Mrs. Bensly we owe the account of how the work was carried on.[1] For the sake of better light the manuscript was carried into the open air, and the three scholars divided the nine or ten hours of daylight into three regular watches. A wash-stand did duty as a writing-desk, and ' a kind of hallowed circle was kept around that little table by day, where no interruption was allowed to intrude, though loving hands were ever ready to sharpen the pencil or refill the

[1] *Our Journey to Sinai* (Religious Tract Society, 1896).

PLATE III.

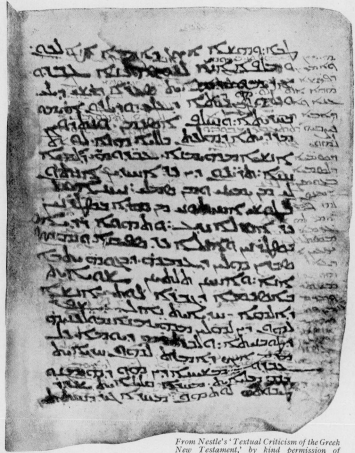

From Nestle's 'Textual Criticism of the Greek New Testament,' by kind permission of Messrs. Williams & Norgate.

A PAGE OF THE SINAITIC SYRIAC PALIMPSEST (THE LEWIS GOSPELS), SHOWING MATT. XV. 12-27.

See p. 68.

inkstand, to hold down the leaves when the wind was high, or reach Bibles and dictionaries that found no place on the narrow board.'

On several other occasions Mrs. Lewis returned to the monastery to verify doubtful readings, and the result is her beautiful facsimile edition of the Codex. Of its value there can be no doubt. Its exact age and its relation to other Old Syriac texts are still matter of discussion, but Mrs. Lewis herself inclines to see in it a copy of the primitive Syriac text, which was in use by the Church in Palestine not later than A.D. 150, or within fifty years of the death of St. John.

The manuscript contains many interesting readings of a Western type, of which the most important is Matt. i. 16 : ' Joseph, to whom was betrothed Mary the Virgin, begat Jesus, who is called the Christ.' At first sight the Syriac text seems to deny the Divine birth of our Lord. And it has been suggested that it was altered to support the view of the Ebionites, who held that our Lord was the human son of a human father, and that the Divine Spirit entered into Him at His baptism. But if this Ebionitic sense was intended, it is strange that the writer should not, at the same time, have altered verses 18 and 20, where the Divine birth is clearly stated. And the probability is

that ' begat ' in verse 16 is to be understood in
an official sense—of an official line of succession
rather than of literal descent. 'The variant
reading, therefore,' according to Sir F. G.
Kenyon's summing up, 'though interesting
(and possibly coming near to the text of the
original document from which St. Matthew's
genealogy was derived, and in which our Lord
would of course be entered as the son of
Joseph), has no important doctrinal bearings '
(*Handbook*, p. 154 f.).

We may note also the omission of ' first-born '
($\pi\rho\omega\tau\acute{o}\tau\epsilon\kappa o\nu$) in Matt. i. 25 in agreement with
the best Greek authorities, and the same applies
to the words ' to be baptized with the baptism
that I am baptized with ' in xx. 22. Interesting,
too, is Mark x. 50 where, in accordance with
Eastern custom, it is said of Bartimaeus that he
' rose, took up his garment and came to Jesus,'
not ' cast it off ' as the ordinary text states. And
have we not a striking example of our Lord's
chivalry when, as Mrs. Lewis points out, in
John iv. 27, His disciples find Him ' standing
and talking with the woman,' instead of sitting,
the usual attitude of a Jewish Rabbi when teaching ? In no other manuscript is He so described, but the fact that He rose to His feet in
speaking to the poor degraded woman is surely
a sign of His innate courtesy. If, too, we can

accept the variant in Mark viii. 31 f. ' and they will kill Him, and the third day He will rise and openly speak the word,' it would imply that our Lord Himself spoke openly after His Resurrection, and not only through the agency of His disciples. Matt. xxiii. 13, again, gives a graphic picture of priestly pretensions : ' But woe unto you, Scribes and Pharisees, hypocrites ! for ye hold the key of the kingdom of heaven before men ; for ye neither enter in, nor those that are coming do ye suffer them to enter.' Or to take one more example—according to the striking reading of Matt. xxvii. 16, the personal name of the robber was the same as our Lord's, so that Pilate's question to the Jews ran, ' Whom will ye that I release unto you ? Jesus Bar-Abba, or Jesus who is called the Christ ? ' [1]

At the end of the Codex is one of the colophons which are so common in ancient manuscripts : ' Here endeth the Gospel of the *Mĕpharrĕshê*, four books. Glory to God and to his Christ, and to his Holy Spirit. Let every one who reads and hears and keeps and does [it] pray for the sinner who wrote [it]. May God in his tender mercy forgive him his sins in both worlds. Amen and Amen.'

[1] For a popular account of the Codex and its variants see *Light on the Four Gospels from the Sinai Palimpsest*, by Agnes Smith Lewis (London, 1913).

The Peshitta.

So much, then, for the Old Syriac versions, but we have still to reckon with the great standard version, the *Peshitta* (or *Peshitto*), a word which is generally supposed to mean ' simple,' perhaps in contrast to Tatian's composite narrative, or as pointing to the ' common ' or ' current ' use of the version, like the Vulgate in the Latin Church.

At one time the Peshitta was believed to be the original translation of the Scriptures into Syriac, but now the majority of modern scholars do not place it earlier than the fifth century, and believe that it is practically a revision of the Old Syriac texts, of which we have been thinking, much as the Vulgate is a revision of the Old Latin texts. As regards its author, Professor Burkitt believes that he was Rabbûla, Bishop of Edessa from 411 to 435, or in any case that the new version was published under Rabbûla's auspices.[1] His biographer distinctly tells us that on his accession to the See ' he translated by the wisdom of God that was in him the New Testament from Greek into Syriac, because of its variations, exactly as it was.' Unlike the Curetonian and Sinaitic versions, which are confined to the four Gospels,

[1] *Early Eastern Christianity* (London, 1904), p. 57.

the Peshitta contains the whole Old Testament, except the Apocrypha, and the whole New Testament, except the Apocalypse and the four minor Catholic Epistles—2 Peter, 2 and 3 John and Jude, though these were afterwards supplied from later versions.

The Peshitta has been the standard version of all branches of the Syrian Church for some fifteen centuries, but it was first edited at Vienna in 1555. A new critical edition of the Gospels by G. H. Gwilliam appeared in 1901, and more recently the British and Foreign Bible Society have issued a convenient edition, including the four minor Catholic Epistles which are wanting in the original Canon.

The Egyptian Versions.

According to tradition Christianity was introduced into Egypt by St. Mark, and the recently discovered fragments of canonical and un-canonical Scripture and the so-called Sayings of Jesus are in themselves proofs of how widely and quickly Christianity was diffused throughout the land.

It is with the native translations, however, that we are alone concerned at present. These were in Coptic, the ancient Egyptian language, which later came to be written in Greek characters with six new letters. Coptic embraced many different dialects, but for our purpose it is sufficient to notice the Sahidic dialect which prevailed in Upper Egypt and the Bohairic in the Delta. Many problems surround the different translations into these dialects, but the probability is that the Sahidic translation came first in the third or fourth century in a district where Greek was already widely known, and that it was followed some centuries later by the more official Bohairic. Of the Sahidic large numbers of fragments have been recovered, while in the Bohairic dialect there are many manuscripts containing complete books of the New Testament. Their text is of great importance seeing, particularly in the case of the Sahidic, that it is closely related to the text of the Vatican Codex, while the fidelity with which the text has been transmitted down the ages is very noteworthy.

Not to linger, however, over these versions, pointed attention must be drawn to one of the most important Egyptian finds in recent years, namely, a very early *Coptic Gospel of St. John*.

In March 1923 representatives of the British School of Archaeology in Egypt were working at Qua-el-Kebir, a spot about one hundred miles north of Thebes and Luxor. Digging some eighteen inches beneath the surface in the vicinity of some Roman graves and Coptic tombstones, one of the explorers came across a rough earthenware jar made of red Nile pottery, in which was a small bundle of papyrus leaves rolled up in a linen rag and tied with thread. The leaves were sent to London to be examined by Sir Flinders Petrie, when they were found to contain almost the whole of a Coptic version of St. John's Gospel, written throughout in a careful and scholarly hand, closely resembling the script of the famous Codex Vaticanus. On this and other grounds the manuscript has been assigned to the third quarter of the fourth century, making it one of the oldest manuscripts containing anything like a complete Gospel in any tongue. An edition in facsimile of Papyrus Q, as it has been named from the place of its discovery, has been brought out by Sir Herbert Thompson under the auspices of the British School of Archaeology in Egypt, with valuable Prolegomena and an English translation following the Coptic text.

The size of the papyrus leaves—eighty-six in all—and other considerations, make it probable that it was a Church copy, while the fact that it is written in a dialect of the Coptic vernacular shows that it was ' a Gospel for common peasants in their own vulgar tongue—a Missionary version in a native language as we would call it to-day.'

Many of its new readings are very interesting. One or two may be quoted from the story of the Crucifixion : John xix. 3, ' And they came unto him saying, Hail, king of the Jews, buffetting him on his face ' ; xix. 23, ' The soldiers who had crucified Jesus took his cloak and they made it in four parts, a part to each one of the soldiers, and also the tunic ; but the tunic was not sewn, but it was a square-woven *piece*.'

As further showing the character of the Version and the closeness of its resemblance to our ordinary text, we may cite a few verses from chapter xx. 19 ff. in Sir Herbert Thompson's translation :

19. But *the* evening of that day, the Lord's day (Lit. the Kyriake), the doors being closed of the place where the disciples were for fear of the Jews, Jesus came, he stood in their midst, he said unto them, Peace unto you. 20. And when he had said this, he showed unto them his hands and his side. The disciples were glad when they saw the Lord. 21. He said therefore again, Peace unto you ; as my Father hath sent me, I also send you. But when he had said this, he breathed in their face ; and he said unto them, Receive the Holy Spirit. 23. Those whose sins ye shall forgive, they shall be remitted

unto them : those whom ye retain theirs, they shall be retained. 24. But Thomas, one of the twelve, called Didymus was not there when Jesus came. 25. The disciples therefore said unto him, We have seen the Lord. But he said unto them, Except I see the marks of nails in his hands and I put my hand to his side, I shall not believe. 26. But after eight days his disciples were within again and Thomas also with them. Jesus came, the doors being closed, he stood in their midst. He said therefore again unto them, Peace unto you. 27. Then he said to Thomas, Reach thy finger to these places and see my hands and reach thy hand and put (Lit. send it (?)) to my side, and be not . . .

Thanks to the generosity of friends of the British and Foreign Bible Society, Papyrus Q has found a home in the Library of the Bible House in London. No place could be more appropriate, as its custodier, Dr. R. Kilgour, points out in his graphic account of the manuscript. ' Ranged on the shelves around it stand more than 17,000 volumes which contain some portion of God's Word printed in over 870 different languages. And in its hoary antiquity it can gaze upon these newcomers—none of them as yet 500 years of age, most of them not fifty—and it can proudly claim to be a fore-runner of them all, a prophecy and herald of what the Bible Society stands for—the Gospel for every man in the language in which he was born.' [1]

Armenian Version.

About A.D. 400, translations of the New Testament were made into Armenian, partly from Greek and partly from Syriac sources, and these were revised about the year 433 with the help of Greek manuscripts from Constantinople, said to be ' accurate and reliable copies.' No manuscripts of the primitive form survive, but one manuscript of the tenth century, now in the Patriarchal Library of Edschmiadzin, inserts before the last twelve verses of St. Mark's Gospel the rubric in small red uncials—' of Ariston the Presbyter.' And Mr. F. C. Conybeare has made the suggestion (Hastings, *D.B.*, i. p. 153) that the reference is to a certain Arist(i)on mentioned by Papias as one of the disciples of the Lord, and consequently that in this Arist(i)on we may find the real author of the close of St. Mark's Gospel, which it will be remembered is left blank in the Vatican and Sinaitic Codices (see p. 37). The suggestion is at least an interesting one, and has gained

---

[1] *Four Ancient Manuscripts in the Bible House Library* (B. and F. Bible Society, London, 1928), p. 38.

the approval of so cautious a critic as the late
Professor Swete in his Commentary on St.
Mark.

The same manuscript contains an account of
the woman taken in adultery, though not in the
usual form :

A certain woman was taken in sins, against
whom all bore witness that she was deserving
of death. They brought her to Jesus (to see)
what he would command, in order that they
might malign him. Jesus made answer, and
said, ' come ye, who are without sin, cast stones,
and stone her to death,' but he himself bowing
his head was writing with his finger on the earth
to declare their sins ; and they were seeing their
several sins on the stones, and filled with shame
they departed and no one remained, but only
the woman. Saith Jesus, ' go in peace, and
present the offering for sins, as in their law is
written.'

It may be added that a Venetian manuscript
of A.D. 1220 contains the books of the New
Testament in the following order, Gospels,
Acts, Catholic Epistles, Revelation of John the
Apostle, the Epistles of Paul, to which is added
the apocryphal letter of the Corinthians to Paul.
The Epistle to the Hebrews precedes those to
Timothy, and follows Thessalonians. We have
thus a striking example of the extent to which
the order of the New Testament books in some

of the old lists differs from what we are accustomed to in our English New Testament.[1]

Gothic Version.

While the Goths were still in Moesia in the
fourth century, their Bishop, Ulfilas, or Wul-
filas, a Cappadocian, translated the whole Bible
into Gothic for them, with the exception of the
books of Kings, which he omitted because of
their warlike character. He himself was an
Arian, but did not allow his doctrinal views to
affect his translation, unless in such a passage
as Phil. ii. 6, where he substitutes ' likeness ' for
' equality ' in the Son's relation to the Father.
On the other hand, it is interesting to note, as
Professor Scott has done in his *Ulfilas : Apostle
of the Goths*, traces in the translation of distinc-
tive Teutonic ideas, as when one word is used
to sum up the notion of guilt and the notion of
debt, or as when the sinner after judgment is
depicted as an outcast and a wanderer, or as
when salvation is regarded as a healing power.

The principal manuscript of Ulfilas' translation, which now exists only in fragments, is the
Codex Argenteus, written in silver letters on
purple-stained vellum. The writing points to
its origin in Northern Italy in the fifth or sixth

[1] See further Milligan *Documents*, p. 292 ff.

century. Thence the manuscript found its way
to the monastery of Werden in Germany, and
in 1648 reached Sweden as part of the booty
taken in the Thirty Years' War. It is now preserved in the University Library at Upsala,
and I well remember the reverential care with
which the librarian unrolled the precious manuscript from its rich coverings when showing it
to me.

Apart from its religious significance, the translation has a wide interest as the ' foundation-
stone ' of all Teutonic literature, as Ulfilas had
actually to devise an alphabet for its expression.
He was consequently the first ' to raise a bar-
barian tongue to the dignity of a literary language, and made for himself and his Goths a
monument even more lasting than their deeds.'
Of the man himself it must be sufficient to recall
that he was summoned to attend the Council of
Constantinople in A.D. 381, but no sooner had
he reached Constantinople than he fell sick,
and before he had put his hand to the task
which had brought him there, ' he was taken
up after the manner of Elias the prophet.'
' Only observe,' says his admiring pupil Auxen-
tius, ' the high desert of the man who by the
hand of God was brought to die at Constantinople, call it rather Christianople, where the
holy and spotless priest of Christ might receive

such strange and brilliant honours at the hands of so great a multitude of Christians.'

Other Versions.

Other Oriental versions, such as the Ethiopic, Arabic, Georgian, Slavonic and Persian, are of a comparatively late date, and may be ignored for our present purpose. But it is different with the great Latin versions of which we have now to speak.

Old Latin Versions.

As in the case of the Syriac versions we found certain Old Syriac translations giving place to the Peshitta, so now behind the Vulgate lie certain Old Latin translations, from which the Vulgate was derived by a process of revision and embellishment.

The early history of these Old Latin versions is wrapped in considerable obscurity. We might have expected that the first traces of them would have been found in Rome, but the early Roman Church, as we have seen (p. 14 f.), was a Greek-speaking Church, and we must look rather to some district removed from the culture of the Capital, and all probability points in the direction of North Africa. There, at any rate, the great Latin Fathers, Tertullian and Cyprian, are found quoting from a Latin translation, or translations, which must have commenced as early as the middle of the second century. Other Latin versions naturally followed in Europe and, as the result of a continuous process of recopying and revision, a great number of variant readings passed into circulation. The remains of these early Latin versions are often very fragmentary, and are usually distinguished by the name of the city or library where they are preserved, and by the small letters of the alphabet. Thus, Codex Vercellensis (*a*) is a fourth century manuscript containing the Gospels in the order Matthew, John, Luke and Mark ; Codex Veronensis (*b*) is a purple-stained manuscript of the fifth century written in silver letters, with such words as God, Jesus Christ, Holy Spirit, in gold ink ; and Codex Bobbienses (*k*) is a sixth century manuscript, which at one time found a home in the Irish monastery of Bobbio in North Italy, and is noteworthy as containing (only) the shorter ending to St. Mark's Gospel (cf. p. 193).

In view of the corruption of text, to which attention has already been drawn, the need of a uniform and authoritative version quickly made itself felt. And with the need came the man to meet it.

The Vulgate.

Eusebius Sophronius Hieronymus, better known as Jerome, was born in A.D. 329 at Stridon in Dalmatia, and died at Bethlehem in A.D. 420. From his early youth Jerome was devoted to Biblical studies, and his knowledge and zeal were readily recognized when after a period of quiet retirement in Bethlehem, his 'Paradise,' he returned to Rome in A.D. 383. His character and his ability brought him under the notice of the reigning Pope, Damasus, who appointed him as his secretary, and afterwards sought his aid in the revision of the Latin text of Scripture which was so urgently required. Jerome accepted the task, though in the famous Letter which he addressed to Damasus he showed his consciousness of the difficulties that lay before him :

Thou dost constrain me to make a new work out of an old one, in that I am to sit in judgment on the Scriptures after they have now become dispersed throughout the whole world, and (because of their variations) to decree what are the readings that agree with the truth which is contained in the Greek text. It is a pious undertaking—but presumptuous and dangerous—to judge for others in a matter that requires the judgment of all, to change the language of an old man and to drag the white-haired world back to childhood's beginnings. For who is there—be he learned or unlearned—who, taking up my volume, and seeing a reading different from that to which he is accustomed, will not straightway burst out in invective against me, and call me a falsifier and sacrilegious for daring to add or change or correct anything in the Ancient Books ? Against malice of this sort, two things console me. The first is that thou, who art the High Priest, commandest the work to be done ; the second is that it is plain —even from the testimony of those who revile me—that that which shews a variation makes a stray from the truth. If they desire me to put faith in Latin MSS., let them tell me which they are ; for scarcely two Latin MSS. are the same. But if we are compelled to seek for the truth among many MSS., why not go back to the original Greek, and with that before us correct what has been faultily translated, or recklessly emended by incompetent revisers, or added or altered by sleepy copyists ? . . .[1]

By the year A.D. 384 Jerome had completed a revision of the Four Gospels, which was, on the whole, very conservative, a fact which doubtless helped its acceptance throughout Latin-speaking Christendom. Other books of the New Testament followed on the same lines, but it was different when Jerome turned to the Old

---

[1] The above translation is taken from *The Records Unrolled*, by E. S. Buchanan (London : Ouseley), p. 15.

Testament. There his revision was far more searching, and was based no longer on the Septuagint, as in the case of the Old Latin versions, but upon the original Hebrew. The changes thus necessitated in many familiar words and phrases led to a storm of abuse, which was met by equally strong language on Jerome's part. ' Two-legged asses ' was among the terms which he hurled at his opponents, who ' mistook ignorance for holiness.' While, as illustrating the popular feeling, it is enough to recall St. Augustine's story of the African Bishop who favoured the new version, and ordered the section on Jonah's gourd to be read from it in the Church. But Jerome had changed ' gourd ' (*cucurbita*) into ' ivy ' (*hedera*), and when the people recognized that this was due to a new translation, they protested so vehemently that the Bishop was obliged to abandon his attempt.

Eventually, however, the Vulgate, or the version ' in common use,' as Jerome's version came to be called, won its way and became the Bible of Western Europe for a period of a thousand years.

We cannot follow its history in detail during this long period, beyond pointing out that we are again met with an ever-increasing corruption of text necessitating further attempts at revision

as in the case of the Charlemagne Bible, prepared by the learned Alcuin at the beginning of
the ninth century.

The Council of Trent in 1546 marked another
definite period in the history of the Vulgate,
when it was laid down ' that this ancient and
vulgate edition, which has been approved by
the long use of so many ages in the Church
itself, shall be esteemed as authentic (*pro
authentica*) in public readings, disputations,
preachings, and expositions, and that no one
may dare or presume to reject it on any pretext
whatever.' [1]

Notwithstanding this it again became so ap-
parent that the text contained many errors that
a revision was resolved upon. It fell to Pope
Sixtus V (1585-90) to carry this through, but
the result was far from satisfactory, and accordingly, after the death of Sixtus, the edition was
called in and a new and revised issue was
ordered by Clement VIII in 1592, which under
the name of the Sixtine-Clementine Vulgate
has come to be recognized as the standard
edition of the Roman Catholic Church. But
again the text was far from satisfactory, leading

[1] For the original text of the Decree see Souter, *Text
and Canon*, p. 236 f., where it is pointed out that *authentica*
is to be taken in relation to other Latin translations which
were in circulation and practically means ' authoritative.'

to the charge that the Vulgate was ' the worst edited and the least known work of Latin literature.' [1] It must, accordingly, be a source of pride to British scholarship that this reproach is in course of being removed by the publication of a definitive critical edition at the hands of the late Bishop John Wordsworth of Salisbury, and the Dean of Christ Church, Oxford, Dr. H. J. White. The Gospels, Acts, and various Epistles of St. Paul have already appeared, and Dr. White has also provided a handy edition of the whole Latin New Testament for general use.

Nor are the Papal authorities behindhand in similar undertakings. Under the direction of Pope Pius X, the Order of St. Benedict was entrusted in 1908 with the task of collecting materials for the recovery of the Latin text as nearly as possible in the original words of Jerome. The task is a stupendous one, owing to the number of manuscripts which have to be collected and collated, but good progress is being made with the work, the first two volumes of which, embracing Genesis, Exodus, and Leviticus, having appeared in the course of the present year. It is also significant that a new Roman Catholic Version of the New Testament, based not on the Vulgate but on the original

[1] See S. Berger, *Histoire de la Vulgate pendant les premiers siècles du moyen âge* (Paris, 1893), p. 16.

Greek, has recently been published,[1] so fully agreed are scholars in all branches of the Christian Church that the most exact study of the sacred letter is necessary, if full understanding is to be reached regarding spiritual truth.

It ought to be mentioned here, as a matter of special interest to us in this country, that what is probably the best single manuscript of the Vulgate, the Codex Amiatinus, was written at Wearmouth or Jarrow early in the eighth century, and was taken to Rome in A.D. 716 as a present for Pope Gregory. It had previously been deposited for a time in the monastery of Monte Amiata, hence its name, and is now one of the glories of the great Laurentian Library at Florence.

The story of the Vulgate will meet us again in connexion with the English translations based upon it. Meanwhile, ' it is enough to remember that the first translators of our Bible had been familiarised with the Vulgate from their youth, and could not have cast off the influence of early association. But the claims of the Vulgate to the attention of scholars rest on wider grounds. It is not only the source of our current theological terminology, but it is,

[1] *The Westminster Version of the Sacred Scriptures*, edited by the Rev. Cuthbert Lattey, S.J., and the Rev. Joseph Keating, S.J. (London : Longmans).

in one shape or other, the most important early witness to the text and interpretation of the whole Bible.'[1]

Patristic Quotations.

As materials towards the recovery of our New Testament text there remain still Patristic Quotations, or, more generally, citations from our New Testament books which are found in early Christian writings. These citations are naturally very numerous, and it is hardly too much to say that if our Greek Manuscripts and Early Versions were lost, we could still reconstruct a large proportion of the New Testament by the aid of Quotations.

We cannot discuss these at length, but it must be noted that certain dangers attend their use. There is, for example, the uncertainty regarding the true text of the writings in which the quotations are found ; there is the difficulty the scribes had in verifying their references, in view of the manuscripts from which they were derived not being divided up into chapters and verses ; and there is the habit of copyists quoting largely from memory or substituting a free rendering for an exact citation.

[1] B. F. Westcott, Art. ' Vulgate ', p. 1689 in Smith's *Dictionary of the Bible*.

Everyone knows the difficulty of accurate quotation. How many would at once detect the errors in such citations as, ' Go thy way for this time, when I have a *more* convenient season, I will call for thee ' (Acts xxiv. 25) ; ' *Diligent* in business : fervent in spirit, serving the Lord ' (Rom. xii. 11), and ' Ye do shew *forth* the Lord's death till He come ' (1 Cor. xi. 26) : while, as proving that the failing is widely spread, Clement of Alexandria is credited with quoting Matt. xviii. 3 in four different ways, and Jeremy Taylor with quoting John iii. 3 nine times, but only twice in the same form, and never once correctly.

Apart from these and other considerations which cannot be entered on just now, Quotations form a valuable additional aid in our enquiry. They come to us from an early date ; they help to fix the time and place at which a particular reading was current ; and in the hands of later critics they play a most important part in determining the type of text which is to be preferred.

Place of Conjecture.

There remains only the consideration whether conjecture is to have any place in the recovery of that text. We know the large part which it has played in the restoration of classical writings and in early English literature. How much, for example, the text of Shakespeare's Plays owes to it, as in the case of Theobald's famous emendation in *Henry V*, Act 2, Scene 3, where it is said of the dying Falstaff that ' a' babbled of green fields,' instead of the meaningless reading in the folio ' and a table of green fields.' Hence the question naturally arises whether we may employ conjecture similarly in connexion with our sacred books. Many critics hold that it is altogether out of place, if only in view of the number and variety of the sources on which we can depend.[1] Nor must it be forgotten that even those critics who adopt the practice freely are amongst the first to admit how often their conjectures are found to be unnecessary in view of fresh light thrown upon the text. In any case, therefore, it is certain that if conjecture is applied it must be with very great caution, and only when all other means for the restoration of the text have failed.

[1] See, for example, Scrivener, *Introd.*[4], ii. p. 244: ' It is now agreed among competent judges that *Conjectural Emendation* must never be resorted to, even in passages of acknowledged difficulty '; and for a different point of view compare Rendel Harris, *Side-Lights on New Testament Research*, pp. 177 ff.

LECTURE IV

CRITICAL EDITIONS OF THE GREEK NEW TESTAMENT

'Sure I am that there cometh more knowledge and understanding of the Scripture by sundry translations than by all the glosses of our sophistical doctors.'

(*Prologue unto the Christian Reader*, Miles Coverdale).

CRITICAL EDITIONS OF THE GREEK NEW TESTAMENT

' Others have laboured, and ye are entered into their labour ' (John iv. 38).

WE HAVE reviewed the materials at our disposal for the recovery of the New Testament text, viz. Manuscripts, Versions, and Quotations. We have now to consider the use made of them. But before doing so let us notice two events which have a direct bearing upon our enquiry.

Revival of Greek Learning.

The first is the revival of Greek learning. By the fall of Constantinople in 1453 Greek scholars were driven westward, and a fresh era began in the study of Greek. ' Greece had risen from the grave with the New Testament in her hand ' (Godwin), and though England did not at first welcome the new learning, by the close of the fifteenth century a band of Greek scholars had congregated at Oxford, including such men as Hugh Latimer, Thomas

More, and John Colet. To these in 1498 came the great Erasmus, who, twelve years later, took up his residence at Cambridge, where he diligently prosecuted his Greek studies in the rooms at Queen's College which are still associated with his name.

Invention of Printing.

The other event is the invention of printing. Up to this time the multiplication of copies of the Holy Scriptures had been by the slow and laborious process of copying by hand, but about the middle of the fifteenth century Fust, a goldsmith of Mainz, perfecting Gutenberg's experiments, issued from the press the first printed Latin Bible, generally known as the Mazarin Bible, from a copy found in the library of Cardinal Mazarin. This is believed to have been the earliest book of any size printed from movable type, and hence Hallam can speak of ' this venerable and splendid volume leading up the crowded myriads of its followers, and imploring, as it were, a blessing on the new art, by dedicating its first fruits to the service of Heaven.' [1] The discovery soon spread, and of the Latin Bible alone over ninety editions had been issued before the end of the century.

[1] *Introd. to Lit. of Europe*, i. p. 157.

Complutensian Polyglott.

A printed Hebrew Psalter appeared in 1477 and a Hebrew Bible in 1488 ; but it is astonishing that about fifty years elapsed before the printing of the Greek New Testament. Various small portions, indeed, including the Hymns of Mary and Zacharias, appeared from time to time, but not till 1514 was a complete Greek Testament printed, though not published. This formed part of the Complutensian Polyglott (so named from Complutum, the modern Alcala), which we owe to the learning and wealth of Francisco Ximenes, the Cardinal Primate of Spain.

His aim is clearly stated in the Preface to his New Testament :

No translation can fully and exactly represent the sense of the original, at least in that language in which our Saviour himself spoke. . . . It is necessary, therefore, . . . that we should go back to the origin of the sacred writings, and correct the books of the Old Testament by the Hebrew text, and those of the New Testament by the Greek text.

Every theologian should also be able to drink of that water which springeth up to eternal life, at the fountain-head itself. . . . Our object is to revive the hitherto dormant study of the sacred Scriptures.[1]

[1] See J. P. R. Lyell, *Cardinal Ximenes* (London, 1917), p. 26 f.

The Polyglott consisted of six volumes, of which Volume V, containing the New Testament text, was dated 10th January, 1514. Its contents were arranged in two columns, the Greek on the left and the Latin Vulgate on the right. The Old Testament, which was not issued till 1522, gives us the Hebrew and the Greek Septuagint with the Vulgate in a centre column, like Jesus, according to the Preface, between the two robbers.

It is not easy to discover the manuscripts on which the text of the New Testament was based. Ximenes himself speaks in his dedication to Leo X of ' very ancient codices both of the Old and New Testaments which Leo had sent, and which had aided them very much in their work.' But it is now generally agreed that the manuscripts were comparatively late, certainly not earlier than the twelfth century. The Polyglott must, however, always enjoy the distinction of being the first edition of the New Testament to be *printed* (though not *published*) in the original Greek. Nor can we leave out of sight the beauty of the Greek type which was employed, modelled on the letters of the best manuscripts of the period.

PLATE IV.

NOVVM IN

strumentũ omne, diligenter ab ERASMO ROTERODAMO
recognitum & emendatum, nõ solum ad græcam ueritatem, ue-
rumetiam ad multorum utriusq; linguæ codicum, eorumq; ue-
terum simul & emendatorum fidem, postremo ad pro-
batissimorum autorum citationem, emendationem
& interpretationem, præcipue, Origenis, Chry
sostomi, Cyrilli, Vulgarij, Hieronymi, Cy-
priani, Ambrosij, Hilarij, Augusti-
ni, una cũ Annotationibus, quæ
lectorem doceant, quid qua
ratione mutatum sit.
Quisquis igitur
amas ue-
ram
Theolo-
giam, lege, cogno
sce, ac deinde iudica.
Neq; statim offendere, si
quid mutatum offenderis, sed
expende, num in melius mutatum sit.

APVD INCLYTAM
GERMANIAE BASILAEAM.

CVM PRIVILEGIO
MAXIMILIANI CAESARIS AVGVSTI,
NE QVIS ALIVS IN SACRA ROMA-
NI IMPERII DITIONE, INTRA QVATV
OR ANNOS EXCVDAT, AVT ALIBI
EXCVSVM IMPORTET.

The Title Page of Erasmus' New Testament of 1516. See p. 99.
The print is taken from a copy in the possession of the University of Glasgow.

Erasmus' Greek Testament.

But apart from its own excellence, the work on the Complutensian Polyglott had an unexpected result. It led in March 1515 to a proposal on the part of Froben, the Basle printer, to Erasmus to bring out a Greek edition of the New Testament to anticipate the publication of Ximenes' Polyglott.[1] Erasmus welcomed the proposal, and with such zeal did he set to work that his edition was completed in less than a year, appearing on 1st March, 1516.

No man could have been better fitted for such a task. Erasmus was the foremost scholar in Europe, and had already spent many years in collating Greek manuscripts of the New Testament, while the spirit in which he worked found eloquent expression in the 'Paraclesis' or 'Exhortation' which he prefixed to his Testament :

. . . The sun itself is not more common and open to all than the teaching of Christ. For I utterly dissent from those who are unwilling that the sacred Scriptures should be read by the unlearned translated into their vulgar tongue, as

[1] In this connexion one gladly recalls the noble reply of Ximenes to his editor Stunica, who had sought to depreciate the Erasmus edition : 'Would God that all the Lord's people were prophets ! Produce better if thou canst ; condemn not the industry of another.'

though Christ had taught such subtleties that
they can scarcely be understood even by a few
theologians, or as though the strength of the
Christian religion consisted in men's ignorance
of it. The mysteries of kings it may be safer to
conceal, but Christ wished his mysteries to be
published as openly as possible. I wish that even
the weakest woman should read the Gospel—
should read the epistles of Paul. And I wish
these were translated into all languages, so that
they might be read and understood, not only
by Scots and Irishmen, but also by Turks and
Saracens. To make them understood is surely
the first step. It may be that they might be
ridiculed by many, but some would take them
to heart. I long that the husbandman should
sing portions of them to himself as he follows
the plough, that the weaver should hum them
to the tune of his shuttle, that the traveller
should beguile with their stories the tedium of
his journey.[1]

It was, however, most unfortunate that the
book was passed so hurriedly through the press.
As Erasmus himself admits : ' it was tumbled
out rather than issued ' (*precipitatum verius
quam editum*). Notwithstanding, too, the boast
that he had used not any sort of manuscript but
' the oldest and most correct copies,' he possessed only about seven manuscripts in all,

[1] The translation is taken from F. Seebohm, *The Oxford
Reformers of 1498* (London, 1867), p. 256.

11323

which, with one exception, were neither early nor valuable. For the Apocalypse, indeed, he had only one mutilated manuscript of the twelfth or thirteenth century, and himself supplied the blanks by retranslation from Latin into Greek. Some words of this retranslation still form the text from which our own Authorised Version is rendered, so that there are actually words in that version which go back for their origin not to St. John, but to Erasmus himself.

A notable feature of Erasmus' work was his Latin translation, printed in parallel columns with the Greek text, and differing in many respects from the Vulgate.

Despite its imperfections, Erasmus' edition soon found widespread acceptance. It was of a more convenient size than the rare and costly Polyglott of Ximenes, of which only six hundred copies were printed. Basle was a convenient publishing centre, and Erasmus' reputation as a scholar was fully established. A revised edition of his Testament, correcting many printers' errors, appeared in 1519, from which Luther's German translation is believed to have been made, and this was followed by a third edition in 1522, notable as containing the famous Trinitarian passage in 1 John v. 7-8.

The history of that text is so interesting that

we may pause over it for a moment. In the Authorised Version the words run : ' For there are three that bear record in heaven, the Father, the Word, and the holy Ghost : and these three are one. And there are three that bear witness in earth, the Spirit, and the Water, and the Blood, and these three agree in one.' But in the Revised Version the words run simply : ' For there are three who bear witness, the Spirit, and the water, and the blood : and the three agree in one.' The Trinitarian reference is thus wholly wanting in accordance with the great mass of Greek manuscript evidence and the evidence of the versions, nor is any Greek Father known to quote the passage, though it would have been of great value to him in arguing on the subject of the Trinity. The interpolated words must have come in from the Latin and are no part of the true text. Erasmus accordingly omitted them in his first two editions, but this raised such an outcry that unfortunately he promised to insert the words if any Greek manuscript containing them was produced. A sixteenth century manuscript now at Trinity College, Dublin—the Codex Montfortianus (Evang. 61)—was found to contain the passage, and true to his promise Erasmus inserted it in his third edition, where it held its place down to the time of the Revised Version.

Other editions of Erasmus' Testament appeared in succeeding years, but the texts they embodied constituted practically a single whole, the later editions not being substantially altered from the earlier. No doubt, owing to the fewness and lateness of the Greek manuscripts which Erasmus consulted, and the haste with which the printing was carried through, his text was marked by many imperfections, but at least it broke down the supremacy so long attached to the Latin version and made the New Testament message itself, or rather Him to whom that message pointed, the final Court of Appeal. Let us listen again to Erasmus in the ' Exhortation ' from which we have already quoted :

. . . If the footprints of Christ are anywhere shown to us, we kneel down and adore. Why do we not rather venerate the living and breathing picture of him in these books ? If the vesture of Christ be exhibited, where will we not go to kiss it ? Yet were his whole wardrobe exhibited, nothing could represent Christ more vividly and truly than these evangelical writings. Statues of wood and stone we decorate with gold and gems for the love of Christ. They only profess to give us the form of his body ; these books present us with a living image of his most holy mind. Were we to have seen him with our own eyes, we should not have so intimate a knowledge as they give of Christ, speaking, healing, dying, rising again, as it were, in our own actual presence.

And, to the same effect, in the Dedication to Leo X, the Pope was reminded of his duty to ' make known to the Christians again the commandments of their Master out of the evangelical and apostolic writings themselves.'

Robert Stephanus.

Erasmus died in 1536, but his work was carried on by Robert Stephanus, who in 1546 and 1549 issued new editions of the Greek Testament, known as the ' O mirificam ' editions, from the opening words of the Preface, which extol ' the marvellous ' liberality of Francis I, at whose expense the Greek type was prepared. According to Dr. C. H. Turner ' no other type has ever combined in so high a degree the characteristics of minuteness, beauty, and legibility.'[1]

Following these editions comes Stephanus' principal contribution to the text of the New Testament, the Royal edition of 1550, which contained a short critical apparatus of variant readings, and which held its own so long that Bentley could ironically say that Pope Stephen's

[1] *The Early Printed Editions of the Greek Testament* (Oxford, 1924), p. 26 f.

text stood as if an Apostle had been his com-
positor. The text was, indeed, practically
identical with the *Textus Receptus* or ' Received
Text,' of which we shall have to speak directly.
A further edition in 1551 was notable as containing the division into verses which is still in
use. According to his son, a large part of the
division was made by Stephanus on the occasion
of a journey on horseback (*inter equitandum*)
from Paris to Lyons. An old scholar thinks
it would have been better done ' on his knees
in his closet.' Certainly, taken as a whole, many
of the verse-divisions are very misleading, and
tend to the Scriptures being regarded as a series
of short sayings all equally important and inspired, rather than as a progressive revelation of
God's dealings with men. It is better, therefore,
that the verse-divisions, if retained, should be
relegated to the margin as in our Revised Version.[1]

Beza.

The work of Stephanus was continued by the
Reformer Theodore de Bèze or Beza (1519-
1605), who published nine editions of the New
Testament between 1565 and 1604, which were
not marked by any material differences of text.

[1] See Additional Note E.—The Verse-Divisions in the
New Testament.

The Elzevirs.

These were followed by certain editions issued from the press of the brothers Bonaventure and Abraham Elzevir ; but the departures from the Stephanus text were again not great, and in the Preface to the edition of 1633 the editors make the proud claim : ' Therefore you have a text now received by all (*textum ergo habes, nunc ab omnibus receptum*).' From this the name ' Received Text ' (*Textus Receptus*) has been given to this whole type of text, as representing the work of Erasmus, Stephanus, Beza and the Elzevirs. Upon it our English Authorised Version rests, but it has, as we have seen, little real textual authority behind it and must give way in many points to a text claiming support from earlier and more reliable witnesses.

The next period in the history of our New Testament text occupies nearly two centuries and is mainly concerned with the accumulation and examination of the best textual authorities then available.

Walton's Polyglott.

The first effort in this direction was due to the labour and learning of an English scholar, Brian Walton, afterwards Bishop of Chester,

who in 1657 published a Polyglott Bible on the
lines of the Antwerp (1569-73) and Paris (1628-
45) Polyglotts. Walton himself was a Royalist,
but the Polyglott was brought out under the
patronage of Cromwell, who allowed the paper
for the purpose to be imported free of duty, and
received in return honourable mention in the
Preface. The permission was afterwards with-
drawn and for the ' republican ' copy a ' loyal '
copy was substituted, with a dedication to
Charles II in some issues.

Walton's fifth volume contained the New
Testament in the Greek text of Stephanus'
edition of 1550, with a selection of readings
from the Codex Alexandrinus (see p. 40) and
other authorities at the foot of the page. The
work was still further extended by John Fell,
Dean of Christ Church and afterwards Bishop
of Oxford, who in 1675 brought out an edition
of the New Testament with a selection of readings from more than one hundred manuscripts.
Fell also makes use of the testimony of Coptic
and Gothic versions, but ignores quotations
from the Fathers.

J. Mill.

More important still was the Greek New
Testament of John Mill, first published at

Oxford in 1707. Mill's text was again the text of Stephanus' 1550 edition, but he appended to it a collation of numerous manuscripts, and versions, as well as the witness of patristic quotations. To the whole he prefixed elaborate Prolegomena containing a perfect mine of information. ' There is nothing,' says Professor C. H. Turner, ' like it in England : I wonder if there is in any other country.' [1] But, containing as it does some 30,000 variant readings, it is not to be wondered at that Mill's Testament was subjected to violent attacks from many quarters.

R. Bentley.

In 1713, for example, Anthony Collins published in London his *Discourse of Free-thinking*, in which he casts doubt on the trustworthiness of the New Testament text in view of this number of variants. He was answered by the famous classical scholar, Richard Bentley (1662-1742), who triumphantly vindicated the rights of criticism, showing the importance of variant readings for the establishment of a genuine

[1] *Printed Editions*, p. 8, n.[1]. Cf. Scrivener, *Introd.*[4], ii. p. 202 : ' Of the criticism of the New Testament in the hands of Dr. John Mill it may be said, that he found the edifice of wood, and left it marble.'

text which does not ' lie in any single manuscript or edition,' but ' is dispersed in them all,
while not even in the worst is one article of
faith or moral precept either perverted or lost.'
In consequence, Bentley was led to plan for
himself an edition of the New Testament based
on the agreement of the Greek and Latin
Vulgate, but unfortunately nothing came of it,
though his *Proposals for Printing* (1720) did
much towards opening up the way for revision
of the standard text. So epoch-making indeed
was his work that Dr. Souter does not hesitate
to say that but for him there would have been
no Lachmann and no Hort.

J. A. Bengel.

In the century following Bentley's death any
progress in textual criticism was principally due
to German scholars, amongst whom we must
name J. A. Bengel (1687-1752), who, disturbed
by Mill's 30,000 variants, resolved to investigate
the subject further for himself.

The result was the confirmation of his evangelical faith along with the recognition of certain
critical principles, which have led sometimes
to his being regarded as the father of modern
criticism. In particular, he was the first to
recognize the need of dividing textual witnesses

into families or groups, a principle which has proved of the utmost value in estimating the true character of our witnesses.

J. J. Wettstein.

With our next name, J. J. Wettstein (1698-1745), there is associated an unfortunate story of theological suspicion and controversy which need not detain us. All that we are concerned with is Wettstein's diligence in collating upwards of one hundred new manuscripts, and in drawing large stores of illustrative material from sacred and profane sources. Wettstein printed the Elzevir text, but added a collection of variant readings from different manuscripts, distinguished by letters (uncial manuscripts) and by numbers (minuscule manuscripts) according to a system still in use (cf. p. 30).

J. J. Griesbach.

A notable advance towards a trustworthy text of the New Testament was made by J. J. Griesbach (1745-1812), who developed Bengel's grouping of his authorities in families or recensions. Among the rules which guided him were such well-known canons of interpretation as that a short reading is likely to be more original than one that is longer, and a difficult reading more likely to be preferred to one that is easier. Hug, the Roman Catholic scholar, who criticized Griesbach's recension theory, paid at the same time a hearty tribute to the character of his work : ' With this work he adorned the evening of a laborious and trustworthy life, and in it he left behind him an honourable memorial, which may perhaps be surpassed in respect to the critical materials it contains (for these are daily increasing), but hardly in regard to delicate and accurate criticism.' The first edition of Griesbach's New Testament appeared in parts between 1774 and 1777, and was followed by a revised edition in 1796-1806.[1]

K. Lachmann.

Griesbach in his turn was followed by Karl Lachmann (1793-1851), a trained philologist, who applied to the New Testament text the same principles which he had employed in con-nexion with classical authors. His resources were limited. The Codex Vaticanus had not yet been placed within the reach of students. The Codex Sinaiticus was still undiscovered. But such faithful use did Lachmann make of

[1] According to Gregory (*Canon and Text*, p. 449) a specially prepared edition was at one time a favourite gift in England from wealthy parishioners to their clergyman.

the materials at his command that, in the words of Dr. Hort, ' for the first time a text was constructed directly from the ancient documents without the intervention of any printed edition, and . . . the first systematic attempt was made to substitute scientific method for arbitrary choice in the discrimination of various readings ' (*Introd.* ², ii. p. 13). The first edition of Lachmann's New Testament appeared in 1831, and this was followed by an improved edition in two volumes in 1842-50.

Tischendorf.

The next is one of the greatest names in the history of New Testament textual criticism. Lobegott Friederich Constantin Tischendorf was born in 1815, his name of Lobegott (' praise God ') being given him when his mother found that her presentiment that he would be born blind was not fulfilled. He entered Leipzig University as a student in 1834, and at once turned his attention to Biblical studies. With the aid of a money grant from the Government of Saxony he was enabled to visit various Libraries in the search of ancient documents.

The result was the publication of an edition of the New Testament in 1841. It took eight years to sell 1500 copies, but the importance of the work gradually made itself felt, and other seven editions followed before 1872, the last of which was greatly influenced by Tischendorf's discovery of the Codex Sinaiticus.

Tischendorf died in 1874 before the completion of the Prolegomena to the eighth edition, which were afterwards published by C. Gaspar René Gregory (assisted by Dr. Ezra Abbot). The influence which Tischendorf exercised upon those who came in contact with him comes out well in a striking tribute which Gregory paid to his master : ' If greatness consists in the unwearying pursuit of one idea, Tischendorf was great. If greatness consists in persistent and successful application to the study of difficult things, Tischendorf was great. If greatness consists in surmounting hindrances and prejudices, scholastic, religious, and national, Tischendorf was great. If greatness consists in the acquaintance with the use of, and the turning to general advantage of, the chief literary treasures of Europe and of the nearer East, Tischendorf was great. If greatness consists in earning the gratitude of the scholars of all lands, Tischendorf was great. And if greatness consists in a participation alike in the favor of prince and scholar, of state and of church, Tischendorf was great.' [1]

[1] *Bibliotheca Sacra*, xxxiii. (Andover, 1876), p. 182 f.

Tregelles.

Along with Tischendorf it is impossible not to mention Samuel Prideaux Tregelles (1813-1875), whose work followed on closely similar lines. It was undertaken under the most adverse circumstances, but with the conviction that ' the New Testament is not given us merely for the exercise of our intellectual faculties,' but, ' as the revelation of God, inspired by the Holy Ghost, to teach the way of salvation through faith in Christ crucified.' The text of Tregelles' New Testament, which appeared in six parts (1857-1872), was based on the most ' Ancient Authorities,' while the devout spirit in which it was conceived is shown again in his own words : ' The student of Scripture, who seeks to use it for the spiritual edification of others, takes a high stand, and engages in a blessed work : to those I make no claim in these textual studies ; but one thing I do claim, to labour in the work of that substructure on which alone the building of God's truth can rest unshaken ; and this claim by the help of God I will vindicate for the true setting forth of His word as He wills it for the instruction of His Church.'

Westcott and Hort.

The same may be said with fresh emphasis of the great Cambridge duumvirate—B. F. Westcott (1825-1901) and F. J. A. Hort (1828-1892). Their work was a joint-work in the best sense of the term. For nearly thirty years they devoted themselves to the study of the New Testament text, at first independently and then together. The result was the publication in two volumes in 1881 of a New Testament with the simple title *The New Testament in the Original Greek*, the first volume being devoted to the Text, and the second, the work of Professor Hort, to an Introduction and Appendix justifying the conclusions to which the editors had come. It is not possible here to enter at length into any description of the principles which they advocated, but following the genealogical method they recognized four types of text. These were respectively the Syrian Group, the Neutral Group, the Alexandrian Group, and the Western Group, and of these, by a skilful use of patristic evidence, they gave the preference to the Neutral Group as representing an unrevised and pure text which was found in a few very ancient authorities, such as the Codex Vaticanus and the Codex Sinaiticus, rather than to the readings found in the late uncials and in the great mass of cursive manuscripts.

The work of Westcott and Hort, or WH as they are usually described, has been freely criticized, and cannot claim to represent the last word in textual science, but it is a marvel of patient scholarship and forms an indispensable starting-point for all subsequent workers.

Revisers' Text.

It remains only to notice the text which underlies the Revised Version of 1881. As clearly stated in their Preface, it was no part of the task of the Revisers to construct a continuous text. At the same time they had to determine which were the more correct readings in difficult passages before they could enter on the work of translation, and their general procedure has been interestingly described by one of their number. After certain preliminary matters had been disposed of, the question was raised whether any *textual* changes, that is readings differing from the Greek text of Stephanus' edition of 1550, were proposed. If any change was suggested, the evidence for and against it was briefly stated by two members of the company, Dr. Scrivener and Dr. Hort, who from their previous studies were specially entitled to speak with authority upon such questions, and who came prepared to enumerate particularly the authorities on either side. Dr. Scrivener opened up the matter by stating the facts of the case and his judgment upon them. Then Dr. Hort brought forward any additional matters that might call for notice, and if differing from Dr. Scrivener's view, gave his reasons and stated his own view. After discussion, the vote of the company was taken and the proposed reading accepted or rejected.[1]

Here we must conclude our survey of the various printed editions of the Greek New Testament.[2] Unavoidably the survey has been little more than a list of names, but it will have served its purpose if it has led to a deeper sense of the labours bestowed on our New Testament text, while confirming Dr. Hort's weighty words that ' in the variety and fullness of the evidence on which it rests the text of the New Testament stands absolutely and unapproachably alone among ancient prose writings. . . .

[1] Adapted from S. Newth, *Lectures on Bible Revision* (London, 1881), p. 119 f.

[2] The stupendous work of H. von Soden, of which so much was expected, has not found favour amongst scholars, and need not detain us : see Lake *Text*[6], p. 77 ff.

The expression of doubt, whenever doubt is really felt, is owing to the paramount necessity for fidelity as to the exact words of Scripture.' [1]

[1] *The New Testament in the Original Greek*, small edition, p. 565.

LECTURE V

THE EARLY ENGLISH VERSIONS

' I call God to recorde agaynst the day we shall appeare before our Lord Jesus, to geue a reckenyng of our doynges, that I neuer altered one syllable of God's Word agaynst my conscience, nor would this day, if all that is in the earth, whether it be pleasure, honour, or riches, might be giuen me ' (*Tyndale to Fryth*).

THE EARLY ENGLISH VERSIONS

' We do hear them speaking in our tongues the mighty
works of God ' (Acts ii. 11).

WE HAVE been following the transmission of
the New Testament from its earliest form in
papyrus rolls down to the printed editions of
to-day, and have seen that from a very early
date the New Testament autographs were exposed to great textual corruption, and that a
large number of variant readings soon showed
themselves. Our object, therefore, in the
interest of accuracy, has been to get behind
these variants to the original text by the aid of
all the evidence we can gather. That evidence,
we saw, consists mainly of Greek Manuscripts
of the original writings, of Ancient Versions
into which these writings were translated, and
of Quotations from the early Christian writers.
We then turned to the use made of these
materials by different editors, and learned how
eventually the text which we owe in the first
instance to Erasmus and his immediate successors, known as the Received Text, has had

to give way to a text depending upon better and more ancient authorities.

The Early Paraphrasts.

Nothing has been said as yet of the English Versions of the New Testament, nor are these strictly speaking in the direct line of descent. They cannot, therefore, be said to furnish much evidence for the recovery of the original text. At the same time, because they are English Versions, and the great majority of the people in this country derive their knowledge of the New Testament from them, they cannot fail to be of the utmost interest, and I propose to deal with them in the present and the closing lectures.

We cannot linger over the introduction of Christianity into this country. It must be enough to notice that when St. Augustine and his followers came to Britain in A.D. 547 they brought the Latin Bible with them, and that consequently it was the basis of those Anglo-Saxon and Anglo-Norman paraphrases which for nearly seven hundred years formed the only vernacular version of Scripture which the people of this country possessed.

The earliest of these Anglo-Saxon paraphrasts was the Saxon cowherd Caedmon. According to the beautiful story preserved by the old historian Bede (*Ecclesiastical History*, iv. 24), Caedmon returned one night to the Abbey at Whitby sad and dispirited because he had not been able to take his part in singing at a banquet. Soon after he fell asleep a visitant appeared to him and said, ' Caedmon, sing some song to me.' ' I cannot sing,' was the surprised answer, ' for that was the reason why I left the entertainment.' ' Nevertheless,' replied the other, ' you shall sing.' ' What shall I sing ? ' he asked. ' Sing the beginning of created things,' was the rejoinder. And thereupon Caedmon began to sing well-uttered verses to the praise of God. In the morning he repeated these to the Abbess Hilda, and all saw that ' heavenly grace ' had been conferred on him, and no sooner had he been taught the whole course of sacred history than he converted it into ' most harmonious verse,' and sweetly repeating the same, made his masters in their turn his hearers.

Caedmon was followed by the greatest scholar of his time in Western Europe, the Venerable Bede (A.D. 674-735), who translated the Apostles' Creed and the Lord's Prayer for the use of the less educated priests, and who, at the time of his death, was engaged on a translation of St. John's Gospel. ' Dear master,' said the boy who was acting as his scribe, ' there is yet one sentence not written.' ' Write quickly,' answered Bede. And when soon after the boy said, ' The sentence is now written,' Bede replied, ' It is well ; you have said the truth. It is ended.' Shortly after, sitting on the pavement of his cell and singing, ' Glory be to the Father and to the Son and to the Holy Ghost,' he departed to the Heavenly Kingdom.

No remains of Bede's translation have come down to us, but a Graeco-Latin manuscript of the Acts of the Apostles, which Bede is known to have used, is shown in the Bodleian Library at Oxford (cf. p. 192).

A royal translator comes next—King Alfred (A.D. 848-901)—to whom we owe a translation of the Ten Commandments under the heading ' Alfred's Dooms.' He is also said to have been the author of a version of the Psalms, and in the Preface to his translation of Gregory's *Pastoral Care* gave expression to the wish that ' all the free-born youth of his people, who possess the means, may persevere in learning, so long as they have no other affairs to prosecute, until they can perfectly read the English Scriptures.' [1]

Other versions followed, including a free rendering of certain Old Testament books by Aelfric, the Grammarian (about A.D. 1000),

[1] Possibly the last words do not mean more than ' read English writing.'

whose object in translating comes out clearly in his homily *On Reading the Scriptures* : ' Whoever would be one with God, must often pray, and often read the Holy Scriptures. For when we pray, we speak to God ; and when we read the Bible, God speaks to us. . . . Happy is he, then, who reads the Scriptures, if he convert the words into action. The whole of the Scriptures are written for our salvation, and by them we obtain the knowledge of the truth.'

A further step in the direction of popularizing the Scriptures was afforded by the appearance of Interlinear Translations, in which the Anglo-Saxon equivalent was inserted above the Latin text. The most notable of these translations are the Lindisfarne Gospels, written in Latin about A.D. 690 by Eadfrith, Bishop of Lindisfarne, in honour of St. Cuthbert. It is believed that the Bishop copied the Gospels from a Latin version which Adrian, the friend of Archbishop Theodore, had brought with him to England in the year A.D. 669. The word-for-word Anglo-Saxon translation was the work of Aldred, a priest of the Holy Isle, about the middle of the tenth century. To avoid risk from the marauding Danes the manuscript was at one time carried off to Ireland by the monks, but after incurring various dangers, including submersion in the sea (it is sometimes said that its pages still bear traces of the salt water), was eventually restored to Lindisfarne. After the dissolution of the monastery in 1534 it was purchased by Sir Robert Cotton, and is now included in the Cottonian Collection in the British Museum.

But important as the work of the Interlinear Translations was, they cannot be said to have done more than familiarize the minds of the people with the leading facts of Old and New Testament history, until such time as they should have the whole Bible in their own hands.

The Wycliffite Versions.

The man to whom this was principally due was John Wyclif, ' the morning star of the Reformation.' Struck by the evils and distresses of his times, Wyclif recognized that what the people most required was a wider acquaintance with the Scriptures. ' Christian men,' so he wrote, ' ought much to travail night and day about text of Holy Writ, and namely [especially] the Gospel in their mother tongue, since Jesus Christ, very God and very man, taught this Gospel with His own blessed mouth and kept it in His life.'

To this task, accordingly, both directly, and indirectly through his scholars and friends, Wyclif devoted himself in order that ' with

God's grace poor Christian men may somedeal [partly] know the text of the Gospel ... and therein know the meek and pure and charitable living of Christ and His Apostles to sue [follow] them in virtues and bliss.' A translation of the greater part of the Old Testament was added by one of his strongest supporters, Nicholas of Hereford, with the result that in A.D. 1382, two years before his death, Wyclif had the joy of seeing the whole Scriptures in the hands of the people in their ' modir tonge.'

Four years later a revised and much improved edition was issued by John Purvey, with a Prologue which illustrates so well the true spirit of the Bible translator that it may be reproduced here almost in full :

A simple creature hath translated the Bible out of Latin into English. ... First, this simple creature had much travail, with divers fellows and helpers, to gather many old Bibles, and other doctors, and common glosses, and to make one Latin Bible sumdel [partly] true. ... And I pray, for charity and for common profit of Christian souls, that if any wise man find any default of the truth of translation, let him set in the true sentence and opening of Holy Writ, but look that he examine truly his Latin Bible. ... Lord God ! since at the beginning of faith so many men translated into Latin, and to great profit of Latin men, let one simple creature of

God translate into English, for profit of English men. . . . Therefore a translator hath great need to study well the sentence, both before and after, and look that such equivalent words accord with the sentence, and he hath need to live a clean life, and be full devout in prayers, and have not his wit occupied about worldly things, that the Holy Spirit, author of wisdom, and knowledge, and truth, direct him in his work, and suffer him not to err. . . . By this manner, with good living and great travail, men may come to true and clear translating, and true understanding of Holy Writ, seem it never so hard at the beginning. God grant to us all grace to know well, and keep well Holy Writ, and suffer joyfully some pain for it at the last! Amen.

The work was not carried through without the bitterest opposition and even danger to life. ' The organ of the devil,' ' the idol of heretics,' ' the storehouse of lies ' were some of the epithets that were hurled against Wyclif, and his teaching was publicly condemned at a Synod held at the Dominican monastery at Blackfriars, London. ' Pontius Pilate and Herod are made friends to-day,' was Wyclif's own bitter comment on the union against him of the Prelates and the Monastic Orders long at deadly feud ; ' since they have made a heretic of Christ, it is an easy inference for them to count simple Christians heretics.'

But he and his fellow-workers found their reward in the eagerness with which the new version was welcomed by all classes of the people. According to Foxe : ' Some gave five marks (equal £40 in our money), some more, some less, for a book ; some gave a load of hay for a few chapters of St. James, or of St. Paul in English. . . . To see their labours, their earnest seeking, their burning zeals, their readings, their watchings, their sweet assemblies . . . may make us now in these our days of free profession, to blush for shame.' [1]

Copies of the Wycliffite versions seem to have penetrated even into Scotland, to judge from the Abbot of Inchcolm's lament in 1408 that several Lollards in Scotland had become possessed of the books of Wyclif, which they kept with ' devlish ' secrecy. Or, take another instance associated with the south-west district of Scotland. Some time before 1500 Murdoch Nisbet of Hardhill, in Ayrshire, had become a Lollard, and in consequence had to flee ' overseas.' In his exile he made ' a copy of the New Testament in writ,' which he brought back with him to Scotland, where, warned by the burning of two of his associates for their adhesion to the new faith, he ' digged and built a vault at the bottom of his house,' and there spent his time

[1] *Acts and Monuments*, vii, p. 419 (ed. Seymour).

' serving God and reading his new book.'
After his death that book was handed down
as a precious legacy to his descendants, and a
few years ago an edition was printed by the Scottish Text Society under the editorship of Dr.
Thomas Law. Its significance is surely great
as the one literary relic of Scottish Lollardy
which has come down to us, while the fact that
the translation into Scots was made from a
Wycliffite version connects it with the first
complete vernacular translation of the Scriptures produced in England.

Contrary to his own expectations, Wyclif
was allowed to die in peace, passing away
quietly at his Rectory of Lutterworth on the last
day of 1384. ' Admirable,' says the old church
historian, Fuller, ' that a hare so often hunted
with so many packs of dogs should die at last
quietly sitting on his form.'

One great defect the Wycliffite versions possessed : they were all made, not from the
original Hebrew or Greek, but from the Latin
Vulgate, and hence were only translations of a
translation. On the other hand, this fact had
its value in showing that this was no new Bible
which was being thrust upon the people, but
the old Bible in a different form.

Writing expressly for the people, the translators used every effort to make their meaning

clear and intelligible, and in consequence many of their renderings impress us still with their freshness and force.

Take these examples from Purvey's revision of St. Matthew : ' The lanterne of thi bodi is thin iȝe ' (vi. 22) ; ' A leche [1] is not nedeful to men that faren wel, but to men that ben yuel at ese ' (ix. 12) ; ' And lo ! a man that hadde a drye hoond ' (xii. 10) ; ' Lo ! my child, whom Y haue chosun, my derling ' (xii. 18) ; ' And the boot in the myddel of the see was schoggid with wawis ' (xiv. 24). Or these, some of whose expressions have an unexpectedly familiar sound to Scottish ears : ' Twey men metten hym, that hadden deuelis, and camen out of graues, ful woode [2] ' (viii. 28) ; ' And loo ! in a greet bire [3] al the droue wente heedlyng in to the see ' (viii. 32) ; ' And he cometh, and fyndith it voide, and clensid with besyms,[4] and maad faire ' (xii. 44) ; ' But thei dispisden, and wenten forth, oon in to his toun,[5] anothir to his marchaundise ' (xxii. 5).[6]

To these examples may be added the Lord's Prayer as it appeared in the later Wycliffite Version :

Oure fadir that art in heuenes, halewid be thi name ; thi kyngdoom come to ; be thi wille

[1] Physician. [2] Mad. [3] Rush. [4] Brooms. [5] Farm.
[6] See further, G. Milligan, *The English Bible*, p. 29 f.

don in erthe as in heuene ; ȝyue to vs this dai
oure breed ouer othir substaunce ; and forȝyue
to vs oure dettis, as we forȝyuen to oure det-
touris ; and lede vs not in to temptacioun, but
delyuere vs fro yuel. Amen.

It will be kept in view that the Wycliffite
Versions existed only in manuscript until 1850,
when they appeared in a magnificent edition of
four volumes quarto edited by the Rev. Josiah
Forshall and Sir Frederic Madden.

William Tindale.

Nearly one hundred and forty years elapsed
between Wyclif and our next translator, William
Tindale (about 1490-1536), and during that
period came the revival of learning and the invention of printing, both of which contributed
largely to the character and success of his work
(cf. p. 95 f.).

It is impossible to sketch even in outline the
romantic story of Tindale's life. It must be
enough that from the hour when in controversy
with a Roman Catholic opponent he exclaimed,
' If God spare my life ere many years I will
cause a boy that driveth the plough shall know
more of the Scriptures than thou doest,' until
the day—6th October, 1536—when he died
a martyr's death at Vilvorde near Brussels,

his whole energies were directed to his self-imposed task. It was in exile that that task was performed, for, as he pathetically remarked, ' there was no place to do it in all England.' Voluntarily, therefore, he left his native land in the early summer of 1524, never to see it again. His movements are somewhat uncertain, but he would seem to have gone first to Hamburg and afterwards to Cologne, where he busied himself secretly supervising the printing of the New Testament in English. Word of how he was occupied reached the ears of a Roman Catholic opponent, Dobneck, or, as he is better known, Cochlaeus, who stirred up opposition to Tindale's work and led to his snatching the precious sheets already printed and, with his assistant William Roy, carrying them off to Worms. There the original quarto edition, begun at Cologne, was finished, and along with it Tindale produced a new octavo edition, like the quarto consisting of 3,000 copies. Copies of both issues—the earliest editions of the New Testament printed in English—were at once forwarded to England in barrels of corn and bales of cloth ; but warning of their coming had already been sent, and thousands of copies were seized and burned at the Old Cross of St. Paul's. It was only what Tindale had expected. ' In burning the New Testament,' he wrote, two years later, ' they did none other thing than that I looked for ; no more shall they do if they burn me also, if it be God's will it shall so be.'

Of the original quarto Testament only one fragment, consisting of the text of Matthew down to the middle of chap. xxii., remains, which was discovered in 1836 by a London bookseller, bound up with a tract of Oecolam-padius. The fragment is now in the British Museum.

Of the octavo there are two copies extant ; one, wanting only the title page, in the Baptist College at Bristol ; the other, more defective, in the library of St. Paul's Cathedral.

The striking Prologue with which the quarto is prefaced shows Tindale's profound sense of responsibility and his determination to supply as correct a translation as possible. It runs as follows :

I have here translated (brethren and sisters most dear and tenderly beloved in Christ) the New Testament for your spiritual edifying, con-solation and solace ; exhorting instantly and beseeching those who are better seen in the tongues than I, and that have higher gifts of grace to interpret the sense of the Scripture and meaning of the Spirit than I, to consider and ponder my labour, and that with the spirit of meekness. And if they perceive in any places that I have not attained the very sense of the tongue, or meaning of the Scripture, or have not given the right English word, that they put to their hands to amend it, remembering that so is their duty to do. For we have not received the gifts of God for ourselves only, or for to hide them ; but for to bestow them unto the honouring of God and Christ, and edifying of the congregation which is the body of Christ.

The Address to the Reader in the 1525 octavo edition is also so significant that we may be pardoned for giving a somewhat lengthy extract from it :

Them that are learned Christianly I beseech, forasmuch as I am sure, and my conscience beareth me record, that of a pure intent, singly and faithfully, I have interpreted it, as far forth as God gave me the gift of knowledge and understanding, that the rudeness of the work now at the first time offend them not ; but that they consider how that I had no man to counterfeit, neither was helped with English of any that had interpreted the same or such like thing in the Scripture beforetime. Moreover, even very necessity, and cumbrance (God is record) above strength, which I will not rehearse, lest we should seem to boast ourselves, caused that many things are lacking which necessarily are required. Count it as a thing not having his full shape, but as it were born before his time, even as a thing begun rather than finished. In time to come (if God have appointed us thereunto) we will give it his full shape, and put out if ought be added superfluously, and add to if ought be overseen through negligence, and will enforce to bring to compendiousness that which is now translated at the length, and to give light where it is required, and to seek in certain places more proper English, and with a table expound the words which are not commonly used, and show how the Scripture useth many words which are otherwise understood of the common people, and to help with a declaration where one tongue taketh not another ; and will endeavour ourselves, as it were, to seethe it better, and to make it more apt for the weak stomachs, desiring them that are learned and able to remember their duty, and to help them thereunto, and to bestow unto the edifying of Christ's body, which is the congregation of them that believe, those gifts which they have received of God for the same purpose.

The grace that cometh of Christ be with them that love him. Amen.[1]

Nor was Tindale long in giving effect to his promise. Revised editions of the New Testament were issued in 1532 and 1534 : ' for that purpose I wrote it, even to bring them to the knowledge of the Scripture.' And elsewhere Tindale pleaded in eloquent and pathetic terms : ' if it would stand with the King's most gracious

[1] For the complete text of Tindale's Prologues see Newth, *On Bible Revision*, p. 137 ff.

pleasure to grant only a bare text of the Scripture to be put forth among his people ... I shall immediately make faithful promise never to write more, nor abide two days in these parts after the same ; but immediately to repair unto his realm, and there most humbly submit at the feet of his Royal Majesty, offering my body to suffer what pain or torture, yea, what death his Grace will, so that this be obtained.'

The self-sacrificing plea was of no avail, and soon afterwards this ' true servant and martyr of God ' was betrayed into the hands of his enemies and thrown into prison. It was from there that he wrote the pathetic letter, the only piece of his own handwriting now extant, asking for a ' warmer coat ' and ' above all ' for his ' Hebrew Bible, Hebrew Grammer, and Hebrew Dictionary, that I may spend my time with that study.' [1]

After suffering an imprisonment of nearly a year and a half, he was first strangled and then burned. His last words were, ' Lord, open the King of England's eyes.'

Of Tindale's worth as a man, and of his unwearied efforts in the cause of Bible translation and Bible diffusion, the little that we have been able to say is sufficient proof. Of his place as a

[1] The letter is given in full in Lovett's edition of Demaus' standard Life of *William Tyndale* (London, 1886), p. 437 f.

scholar it must be enough that, while his version undoubtedly bore traces of the influence of the Wycliffite versions at home and of Luther's New Testament in Germany, he was too good a linguist to be slavishly dependent on any one, and can justly claim the credit of being the first in England at any rate (with the possible exception of Bede, cf. p. 192) to go straight to the Hebrew and Greek originals. While as showing in turn the extent of his influence upon the future history of our Bible, it has been calculated that in the whole of his New Testament there are not more than 350 words which do not occur in the Authorised Version, and many of the latter's most happy phrases and sentences are directly traceable to the old translator.

No doubt Tindale's version had its faults, noticeable among them his love, for the sake of variety, of rendering the same Greek word in different ways, a fault in which he was followed by the translators of the Authorised Version. But take his work all in all, and Fuller's eulogy is not exaggerated : ' What he undertook was to be admired as glorious ; what he performed, to be commended as profitable ; wherein he failed, is to be excused as pardonable, and to be scored on the account rather of that age, than of the author himself.' Or in the eloquent words of Mr. Froude : ' The peculiar

genius—if such a word may be permitted—
which breathes through it—the mingled tenderness and majesty—the Saxon simplicity—
the preternatural grandeur—unequalled, unap-
proached in the attempted improvements of
modern scholars—all are here, and bear the
impress of the mind of one man, William
Tyndal.'

It is not possible to illustrate at length
Tindale's influence on those who succeeded
him, but as showing how he laid down the lines
of all subsequent English translations we may
insert his version of the Lord's Prayer, the first
to appear in an English printed Testament :

Matt. vi. 9-13.

O oure father which art in heven halowed be
thy name. Let thy kyngdom come. Thy wyll
be fulfilled as well in erth as hit ys in heven.
Geve vs this daye oure dayly breade. And forgeve vs oure treaspases even as we forgeve them
whych treaspas vs. Lede vs nott in to tempta-
cion but delyvre vs from yvell. Amen.

To this may be added the 1534 version of

Phil. ii. 5-11.

Let the same mynde be in you that was in
Christ Iesu : which beynge in the shape of God,
and thought it not robbery to be equall with
God. Nevertheless he made him silfe of no

reputacioun, and toke on him the shape of a servaunte, and became lyke vnto men, and was founde in his aparell as a man. He humbled him silfe and became obedient vnto the deeth, even the deeth of the crosse. Wherefore God hath exalted him, and geven him a name above all names : that in the name of Iesus shuld every knee bowe, bothe of thinges in heven and thinges in erth and thinges vnder erth, and that all tonges shuld confesse that Iesus Christ is the lorde vnto the prayse of God the father.

Miles Coverdale.

The work which Tindale had so faithfully inaugurated was continued by Miles Coverdale (1488-1569), who is described as ' from his childhood given to learning ' and ' set to the most sweet smell of holy letters.' He had assisted Tindale in his translation of the Pentateuch and, thereafter, urged on by his ' singular good master,' Thomas Cromwell, devoted himself so diligently to the task of Bible translation that at Zurich in 1535 the first complete Bible printed in English was issued from the press.

In his Dedication to Henry VIII Coverdale modestly disclaims the position of an independent translator, and speaks of having ' purely and faythfully ' followed ' fyue sundry interpreters,' who are generally identified with

Luther, the Zurich Bible, the Vulgate, the Latin version of Pagninus, and above all Tindale. At the same time he was very far from being a mere ' proof-reader or corrector ' of the labour of his predecessors. His work possesses un-doubted original value ; and if Tindale in his translation ' gave us the first great outline distinctly and wonderfully etched,' Coverdale ' added those minuter touches which soften and harmonize it.' [1]

It is sufficient to appeal to the version of the Psalms which still appears in the English Prayer Book, and which has come down to us from Coverdale through the Great Bible. In its ' in-comparable tenderness and sweetness,' Bishop Westcott claims to find the translator's own gentle spirit reflected, ' full of humility and love . . . and therefore best in harmony with the tenor of our own daily lives.'

Before leaving Coverdale's Bible, it may be well to recall that he included in it a complete translation of the Apocrypha, prefaced by a most interesting Address : ' These books (good reader) which be called Apocrypha are not judged among the doctors to be of like reputa-tion with the other Scripture . . . But whoso-ever thou be that readest Scripture, let the Holy Ghost be thy teacher, and let one text

[1] See Eadie, *The English Bible*, i. p. 302.

expound another unto thee.' And then, almost by way of apology, he tells us that he has included ' the prayer of Azarias, and the sweet song that he and his two fellows sung in the fire . . . for their sakes also that love such sweet songs of thanksgiving.' In Coverdale's second folio edition of 1537 the Apocrypha are described as ' The books and treatises which among the fathers of old are not reckoned to be of like authority with the other books of the Bible, neither are they found in the Canon of the Hebrew.'

Thomas Matthew.

Coverdale was followed by Thomas Matthew, or as he is also known, John Rogers, the protomartyr of the Marian persecution, who in 1537 brought out a volume containing the best work of Tindale and Coverdale.

Like the second edition of Coverdale's Bible this new version bears to be

Set forth with the Kinges most gracyous licéce,

while Cranmer wrote to Cromwell urgently entreating him to use his influence to get from the King a ' licence that the same may be sold and read of every person . . . until such time that we the Bishops shall set forth a better translation,

which I think shall not be till a day after Domes-
day.' The petition was granted, and hence it
came about that ' by Cranmer's petition, by
Crumwell's influence, and by Henry's authority,
without any formal ecclesiastical decision the
book was given to the English people, which is
the foundation of the text of our present Bible.
From Matthew's Bible—itself a combination of
the labours of Tindale and Coverdale—all later
revisions have been successively formed.' [1]

The Great Bible.

There is yet another Bible which again owed
its inception to the great minister of Henry VIII,
Thomas Cromwell. Not satisfied with any of
the existing versions, Cromwell called in the aid
of Coverdale, who set to work to prepare a
version which might rank as a National Bible.
The work of printing was begun in Paris, but
before it was completed the Inquisition stepped
in, and it was with great difficulty that the
precious sheets were saved and the presses sent
over to England. And as ' four great dry
vatsfull ' of the sheets were also recovered
from a haberdasher to whom they had been sold
' to lap his caps in,' the work was soon finished,
and in April, 1539, The Great Bible, so called

[1] Westcott, *English Bible*[3], p. 71 f.

from its size, was issued from the press. The title of the first edition ran as follows :

The Byble in Englyshe, that is to saye the content of all the holy scripture, bothe of ye olde and newe testament, truly translated after the veryte of the Hebrue and Greke textes, by ye dylygent studye of dyuerse excellent learned men, expert in the forsayde tongues. . . . 1539.

Surrounding the title was an elaborate design attributed to Holbein, in which King Henry VIII is represented seated on his throne, engaged in handing ' the Word of God ' to Cranmer and other clergy on his right hand and to Cromwell and other lay-peers on his left. Below this a preacher harangues a crowd from a pulpit in the open air, from the words, ' I exhort, therefore, that first of all supplications, prayers, thanksgivings, be made for all men, for Kings.' At the mention of kings all shout *Vivat Rex*, or ' God save the King.'

In the following year a second edition of the Great Bible appeared, which is often described as Cranmer's Bible from the Address with which he prefaced it, and to it the following story is probably to be referred. The King had submitted the Bible to divers Bishops to peruse, and, on their being asked what was their judgment of the translation, ' they answered that there were many faults therein.' ' Well,' re-joined the King, ' but are there any heresies maintained thereby ? ' The Bishops replied that there were none that they could find. ' If there be no heresies,' said the King, ' then, in God's name, let it go abroad among our people.'

In consequence, every effort was made to get the people to accept the new version, and copies were attached by chains to the pillars of the churches with the King's injunction that they should be read with ' Discretion, Honest Intent, Charity, Reverence, and Quiet behaviour.' In Old St. Paul's and elsewhere it was a common sight to see an eager crowd gathered round the chained Bible, while some one more educated than the others read aloud. ' Even little boys,' the chronicler tells us, ' flocked among the rest to hear portions of the Holy Scriptures read.'

It must not be thought, however, that this open reading of the Scriptures was everywhere viewed with favour. Thus, to confine ourselves to what took place in Scotland, on 1st March, 1539, through the influence of Cardinal Beaton, five persons were burnt on the Castle Hill of Edinburgh, apparently for no other crime than that they ' did not hesitate to study the books both of the Old and New Testament.' This state of matters was not long allowed to continue. In 1543 it was proposed in the

Parliament meeting at Edinburgh that ' all the lieges in this realm may read the Scriptures in our native tongue,' and proclamation to that effect was duly made at the Market Cross. And so eagerly was the privilege taken advantage of, that twenty-five years later John Knox in describing the effects of this Act was able to write : ' This was no small victory of Christ Jesus, fighting against the conjured enemies of His verity : not small comfort to such as before were holden in such bondage that they durst not have read the Lord's Prayer, the Ten Commandments, nor Articles of their faith in the English tongue, but they should have been accused of heresy. . . . THEN might have been seen the Bible lying almost upon every gentleman's table. The new Testament was borne about in many men's hands.'

The Genevan Versions.

For our next versions we must turn again, as in the case of Tindale, to the Continent.

Owing to the troublous times following the accession of Queen Mary, a body of Reformers sought refuge in Geneva, the city of Calvin and Beza. They found themselves at once in an atmosphere of Bible study, and decided that nothing could be ' more acceptable to God, and comfortable to His Church, than in the trans-

lating of the Scriptures into our native tongue.'
The result was the issue in 1557 by one of their
number, William Whittingham, of a translation
of the New Testament, which according to the
title page had been ' conferred diligently with
the Greke and best approued translations.'
There is also on the title a woodcut of Truth
and Time with the explanation ' God by Tyme
restoreth Trvth and maketh her victorious.' In
addition, Whittingham adopted various expedi-
ents to make the text more generally acceptable
to the ' simple lambs ' for whom it was specially
designed. Roman type was adopted in preference to black letter type. Italics were used to
mark words for which no equivalent existed in
the original Greek text, though they were
required in English to complete the sense,
verse-divisions appeared for the first time in an
English Testament (cf. p. 105), and a marginal
commentary was added, in which the writer
claimed that he had ' omitted nothing unex-
pounded, whereby he that is anything exercised
in the Scriptures of God, might justly complain
of hardness.' The edition may, therefore, claim
to be in a sense the first critical edition of the
New Testament in English, and paved the way
for the translation of the whole Bible which
appeared at Geneva three years later.

In the production of this Genevan Bible

Whittingham was assisted by Thomas Sampson and Anthony Gilby, and the result was a version of admitted excellence which exercised great influence upon subsequent versions. The cost of the work was defrayed by members of the congregation at Geneva *whose heartes God . . . touched* to encourage the revisers *not to spare any charges for the furtherance of such a benefite and fauour of God*. The Genevan version speedily established itself in popular regard, at least 140 editions appearing between 1560 and 1644. Its popularity was due partly to its compact form, and partly to the numerous explanatory notes, which were often of a bitterly anti-papal character, while others were afterwards condemned by King James I as ' partial, untrue, seditious, and savouring too much of dangerous and traitorous conceits.' By way of illustration he cited the notes on Exodus i. 19, which ' alloweth disobedience unto the King ', and on 2 Chronicles xv. 16, which ' taxeth Asa for deposing his mother only ; and not killing her.'

The Bible was prefaced as in the case of so many of these old versions by an instructive address

TO OUR BELOVED IN THE LORD,
THE BRETHREN OF ENGLAND,
SCOTLAND, IRELAND, ETC.   GRACE MERCIE AND PEA
CE, THROUGH CHRIST JESUS.

In it, after speaking of previous translations as requiring greatly ' to be perused and re-formed,' the revisers went on to speak of the advantages they themselves enjoyed ' by reason of so many godly and learned men, and such diversities of translations in divers tongues.' ' And this,' they continued, ' we may with good conscience protest, that we have in every point and word, according to the measure of that knowledge which it pleased Almighty God to give us, faithfully rendered the text, and in all hard places most sincerely expounded the same.'

The Genevan Bible, or the ' Breeches ' Bible, as it was popularly called from the rendering of Genesis iii. 7, ' they sewed fig tree leaves to-gether and made themselves breeches,' [1] was the first Bible to be printed in Scotland (Old Testa-ment, 1579 ; New Testament, 1576), and is usually described as the Bassandyne Bible from the name of the printer of the New Testament. Its price was fixed by the General Assembly at £4. 13s. 4d. pennies Scottis (equal £4 to-day), and by an Act of the Scots Parliament every householder possessed of a certain sum was bound to have a copy, under the penalty of ten pounds.

---

[1] The rendering is also found in Caxton's *Golden Legend* and in Wyclif.

The Bishops' Bible.

It was not to be expected, however, that the successors of Cromwell and Cranmer could look with favour on a translation coming from the school of Calvin, and containing so many ' prejudicial notes.' Accordingly, in 1563-64 Archbishop Parker set on foot a scheme for the revision of Coverdale's version ' to draw to one uniformity.' For this purpose he sorted out ' the whole Bible into parcels ' and distributed these amongst qualified scholars ' to peruse and collate.' The result was published in 1568, and came to be known as the Bishops' Bible from the number of Bishops engaged on it. It contained many marked improvements, pointing to a careful study of the original text, but from its method of production the work was necessarily unequal, and the version owed its position to external authority rather than to its own independent merits. In outward appearance the volume was a splendid folio brought out with every attraction of paper and printing.[1] In 1571 Convocation ordered that a copy should be placed (along with Foxe's *Book of Martyrs*) in every Cathedral and so far as possible in

[1] In a letter to Cecil the Primate drew attention to the fact that ' the printer hath bestowed his thickest paper on the New Testament because it shall be most occupied.'

every Church, and every Archbishop and Bishop was also required to have a copy in his house and to place it ' in the hall or large dining-room, that it might be useful to their servants or to strangers.'

The Rheims New Testament.

Following, as we have been doing, the appearance of our New Testament versions in chronological order, we come to the Rheims New Testament of 1582, the work of certain English Roman Catholics who had sought refuge on the continent during Queen Elizabeth's reign. In keeping with the attitude of the Roman Church to the Latin Vulgate (cf. p. 87), the New Testament bore to be ' translated faithfully into English out of the authentical Latin,' though at the same time the writers claimed that it was ' diligently conferred with the Greek and other editions in divers languages.' The extreme literalness at which the translators aimed, ' word for word and point for point,' led to many stilted renderings and to the use of various Latinized terms which were themselves in need of translation. As examples we may cite : ' Give us this day our supersubstantial bread ' (Matt. vi. 11) ; ' He was assumpted ' (Acts i. 2) ; ' Purge the old leaven that ye may be a new paste, as you are azymes. For our Pasche, Christ, is immolated ' (1 Cor. v. 7).

Of greater interest than those verbal curiosities, most of which have disappeared in subsequent issues, are the renderings in which the writers' theological opinions appear. For example, ' Do penance : for the kingdom of heaven is at hand' (Matt. iii. 2), and 'Blessed are they that hunger and thirst after justice : for they shall have their fill ' (Matt. v. 6). Otherwise the version, though not specially recommended to King James's revisers, influenced them considerably and supplied them with many significant renderings and happy arrangements of words. In the 1st Epistle of John the following phrases are traceable directly to the influence of the Rhemish Version : ' Confess our sins ' (i. 9), where previous versions have ' knowledge ' or ' acknowledge '; ' He is the propitiation ' (ii. 2), instead of ' He it is that obtaineth grace '; ' the unction ' (ii. 20), instead of ' ointment '; and ' we may have confidence ' (ii. 28), instead of ' we may be bold '[1]

Apart from this Roman Catholic version, we are met at the beginning of the seventeenth

---

[1] See especially the monograph by Dr. J. G. Carleton, *The Part of Rheims in the Making of the English Bible* (Oxford, 1902).

century with three versions of the Bible in more or less general use. There was the Great Bible of Henry VIII, still to be seen chained to the desk in many country churches ; there was the Genevan Bible, the favourite Bible of the people ; and there was the Bishops' Bible, supported by ecclesiastical authority. Such a state of things could not, however, continue, and the way lay open for the advent of a new version, which was gradually to supersede all its rivals, and to become for three centuries the Bible of all English-speaking peoples.

LECTURE VI

THE AUTHORISED AND REVISED
VERSIONS

' To whom was it ever imputed for a fault (by such as were wise) to go over that which he has done, and to amend it when he saw cause ? If we will be sons of the truth, we must consider what it speaketh, and trample upon our own credit, yea, and upon other men's too, if either be any way a hindrance to it.'

(*The Translators to the Reader*, 1611.)

THE AUTHORISED AND REVISED VERSIONS

'Finally, brethren, pray for us, that the word of the Lord may run and be glorified' (2 Thess. iii. 1., R.V.).

Origin of the Authorised Version.

WE HAVE traced the history of the early English versions of the New Testament and have noted the repeated attempts to get as faithful a rendering as possible of the original text by means of a series of revisions. Of these revisions three were in common use at the beginning of the seventeenth century : The Great Bible, The Genevan Bible, and The Bishops' Bible, but we can understand the desire to have a new and authoritative version which would gradually supersede all its rivals and become the Bible of all English-speaking peoples. Nor was this desire long in being met, by the appearance of what came to be known afterwards as The Royal Version, or King James's Version. It is strange how little is known regarding the origin of this great version, but it is generally traced to an incident at the

Conference at Hampton Court which the King
held at the beginning of 1604 to hear and determine ' things pretended to be amiss in the
Church.' In the course of the proceedings the
Puritan leader, Dr. John Reynolds, threw out
the suggestion ' that there might be a new
translation of the Bible, because those which
were allowed in the reign of King Henry VIII
and Edward VI were corrupt and not answerable
to the truth of the original.' It is interesting to
notice, however, that, so far at least as the King
was concerned, the way had been prepared three
years before by certain proceedings at a meeting
of the General Assembly of the Church of
Scotland at Burntisland, in 1601, at which he
was present. On that occasion a similar proposal ' for a new translation of the Bible, and
the correcting of the Psalms in meeter,' was
thrown out, and the historian Spottiswood has
told us that ' his Majesty did urge it earnestly,
and with many reasons did perswade the undertaking of the work, showing the necessity and
the profit of it. . . . Speaking of the necessity,
he did mention sundry escapes [errors] in the
common Translation, . . . and when he came
to speak of the Psalmes, did recite whole verses
of the same, shewing both the faults of the
meeter and the discrepance from the text. It
was the joy of all that were present to hear it,

and bred not little admiration in the whole Assembly.' [1] And though nothing further came of this at the time, the King did not lose sight of the suggestion, and we can understand the eagerness with which at Hampton Court he fell in with Reynolds' suggestion and expressed the wish that ' some special pains should be taken in that behalf for one uniform translation . . . professing that he could never yet see a Bible well translated in English ; but the worst of all his Majesty thought the Geneva to be.'

Work of Translation.

Nor was this all, but James showed an active interest in the work by proposing that the new translation should be undertaken by ' the best learned men in both universities, after them to be reviewed by the bishops and the chief learned of the Church ; from them to be presented to the Privy Council, and lastly to be ratified by his royal authority. Furthermore, the King ordered that the whole Church of the Kingdom should be bound by this new translation and none other.'

Notwithstanding the Royal favour bestowed

[1] *History of the Church of Scotland* (Edinburgh edition, 1850), iii. p. 98.

on it, the actual work of revision did not commence until 1607, when the forty-seven (the number originally was fifty-four) Translators appointed for the purpose were divided into six companies, of which two sat at Westminster, two at Oxford and two at Cambridge. These companies met both separately and from time to time together to hear and to compare translations, and the whole was then finally revised by a select company of six or twelve members.

Amongst the men appointed for the task were several justly famed for their scholarship, such as John Reynolds, whose ' memory and reading were near to a miracle ' ; Launcelot Andrewes, of whom it was said that he might have been ' interpreter-general at Babel ' ; Miles Smith, the author of the Preface, who ' had Hebrew at his finger-ends ' ; and Andrew Downs, described as ' one composed of Greek and industry.'

Fourteen rules were laid down for the Translators' guidance, of which the most important were to the effect that the Bishops' Bible should be taken as their basis, but with liberty to use other versions where they were preferable ; that the old ecclesiastical words should be retained ; that there be no marginal notes, except for necessary explanations of Hebrew and Greek words ; and that there should be mutual consultation between the different companies.

PLATE VI.

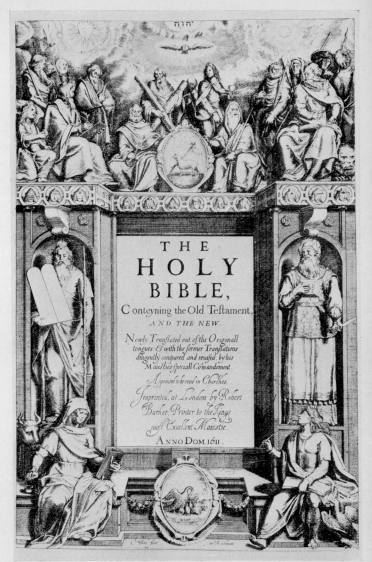

THE TITLE PAGE OF THE 1611 EDITION OF THE AUTHORISED VERSION.

In addition to the figures of the Apostles and Evangelists, note the Incommunicable Name at the head of the page, the Dove, the Triumphant Lamb, and the Pelican feeding her young. See p. 161.

According to a well-known anecdote contained in Selden's *Table Talk*, the general procedure was as follows : ' That Part of the Bible was given to him who was most excellent in such a Tongue, (as the *Apocrypha* to *Andrew Downs*) ; and then they met together, and one read the Translation, the rest holding in their Hands some Bible either of the learned Tongues, or *French*, *Spanish*, *Italian*, etc. ; if they found any Fault, they spoke, if not he read on.'

According to the Translators' own account the whole work was carried through in two years and a quarter, and in 1611 the Bible appeared with the title :

The Holy Bible, Conteyning the Old Testament and the New : Newly Translated out of the Originall tongues ; and with the former Translations diligently compared and reuised by his Maiesties speciall Commandement. Appointed to be read in Churches.

Imprinted at London by Robert Barker, Printer to the King's Most Excellent Maiestie. Anno Dom. 1611. Fol.

In What Sense Authorised ?

It will be noticed that the word ' Authorised,' by which the new version has come to be known, is no part of the title, and, as a matter of fact, there is no evidence that the version was ever publicly sanctioned by Convocation or by Parliament or by the King. Only slowly, and by the force of superior merit, did King James's version attain its commanding position. It became the ' Authorised ' version simply because it was the best.

Nor was it strictly speaking a new translation, and in their interesting Preface, no longer printed in our ordinary Bibles, the Translators specially guard against such an idea. ' Truly,' they write, ' good Christian Reader, we never thought from the beginning that we should need to make a new translation, nor yet to make of a bad one a good one . . . but to make a good one better, or out of many good ones one principal good one, not justly to be excepted against ; that hath been our endeavour, that our mark.' ' Neither did we disdain,' so they continue, ' to revise that which we have done, and to bring back to the anvil that we have hammered . . . fearing no reproach for slowness nor praise for expedition.'

Excellence of the Version.

Of the success of their work it is not necessary to say anything, but we must not imagine that at the time the new version found a ready welcome. One eminent scholar went the length of saying that he ' had rather be rent in pieces by wild horses than any such translation, by my consent, should be urged on poor churches.' If, however, the new version was slow in establishing itself, the hold which, once acquired, it has since maintained is unparalleled in the history of any other English translation.

None have been more ready to admit this than the men who in 1870 were appointed to revise it. ' We,' so the New Testament Revisers tell us in their Preface, ' have had to study this great Version carefully and minutely, line by line ; and the longer we have been engaged upon it the more we have learned to admire its simplicity, its dignity, its power, its happy terms of expression, its general accuracy, and, we must not fail to add the music of its cadences and the felicities of its rhythm.' And one of the most distinguished of their number, Bishop Westcott, who is also the historian of the English Bible, has written : ' Our version is the work of a Church and not of a man. Or rather, it is a growth, and not a work. Countless external influences, independent of the actual translators, contributed to mould it ; and when it was fashioned the Christian instinct of the nation, touched, as we believe, by the Spirit of God, decided on its authority.' He adds—and the words have an important bearing on our present subject : ' Our Bible in virtue of its past is capable of admitting revision, if need be, without violating its history. As it gathered into itself, during the hundred years in which it was forming, the treasures of manifold labours, so it still has the same assimilative power of life.'

Schemes for Further Revision.

From the first, indeed, revision in some form or other marked the history of our Authorised Version. Thus, in 1645, Dr. John Lightfoot, preaching before the House of Commons, urged them to think of a review and survey of the translations of the Bible, and pleaded for a new translation which should be ' exact, vigorous and lively.' And, a few years later, the Long Parliament actually made an order that a Bill should be brought in for a new translation which, however, came to nothing owing to the Parliament's dissolution.

Individual attempts at revision were also forthcoming, one or two of which may be referred to if only to show how readily in some cases they exhibit almost all the features a translation ought not to possess.

In 1764 a *New and Literal* translation of the whole Bible was made by a Quaker, Anthony Purver, prefaced by certain remarks on translations in general, in which he dwells on the

' obsolete, uncouth, clownish' expressions which disfigure the Authorised Version. And this was followed in 1768 by Harwood's translation, written, it is claimed, ' with freedom, spirit, and elegance,' but containing such renderings as : ' The young lady is not dead ' (Mark v. 39) ; ' A gentleman of splended family and opulent fortune had two sons ' (Luke xv. 11) ; ' The clergyman said, you have given him the only right and proper answer ' (Mark xii. 32).

A more ambitious scheme was outlined by a Roman Catholic scholar, Dr. Alexander Geddes, in his *Prospectus of a New Translation of the Holy Bible* (Glasgow, 1786), in which he points out that ' the first and principal cause of the imperfection of almost all modern Translations of the Bible is to be sought for in the imperfection and incorrectness of the originals, from which they were made ; for, when the text to be translated is itself corrupted, the translation must necessarily participate of its corruption ; but modern translations of the Bible have, almost all, been made from a text in many places corrupted : How then could they fail to be, at least, equally faulty ? ' (p. 2). Unfortunately Geddes' own translation had not got further than 2 Chronicles, when it was stopped by the translator's death.

Other translations of the New Testament, in whole or in part, continued to appear, and along with Archbishop Trench's Essay *On the Authorised Version of the New Testament* (1858), Bishop Ellicott's *Considerations on the Revision of the English Version of the New Testament* (1870), Bishop Lightfoot's Essay *On a Fresh Revision of the English New Testament* (1871), and similar books, prepared the way for the *Revised New Testament* of 1881.

Need of Revision.

The need of revision was obvious. Thus, it is now generally recognized that from 1611 to 1614 two sets of copies were already in circulation, differing in many minute particulars and characterized as the ' He ' or the ' She ' Bibles according as they rendered Ruth iii. 15. ' . . . he went into the city ' or ' . . . she went into the city.' Apart, however, from such typographical variations,[1] many of the English words in the Authorised Version had become antiquated, or in the course of three centuries had so changed in meaning as no longer to be understood in the manner that was at first intended.

[1] Another edition was known as the ' Wicked Bible,' because it omitted the ' not ' in the Seventh Commandment. The printers are said to have been fined £300 for the error.

A very commonly cited instance is the familiar precept, ' Take no thought for your life, what ye shall eat or what ye shall drink ' (Matt. vi. 25), which at first sight seems to conflict strangely with the well-established rules of prudence and thrift. But in old English ' thought ' had a note of anxiety attached to it which it has lost, and, therefore, to bring out the full force of the original we require now to render with the Revised Version, ' Be not anxious for your life, what ye shall eat or what ye shall drink,' and similarly in Phil. iv. 6, ' In nothing be anxious ; but in everything by prayer and supplication with thanksgiving let your requests be made known unto God.' In like manner ' occupy ' is no longer generally understood in its old sense of ' employ,' ' trade,' so that it is properly replaced by the latter term in the Parable of the Pounds, ' Trade ye herewith until I come ' (Luke xix. 13). When, again, St. Peter speaks of unbelieving husbands being ' won by the conversation of the wives,' it is the wives' whole ' behaviour ' and not the mere fact of what they say that he has in mind (1 Pet. iii. 1). Similarly, in 1 Thess. iv. 15, ' We which are alive, and remain unto the coming of the Lord, shall not prevent them which are asleep '—' prevent ' is to be understood in its original sense of ' precede ' (cf.

Matt. xvii. 25). Just as, to take an even more striking instance, in Rom. i. 13, ' I purposed to come unto you (but was let hitherto),' where ' let ' means ' hinder,' the very opposite of ' permit ' or ' allow,' as in the modern usage of the word (cf. 2 Thess. ii. 7).

But apart from such changes of meaning in the ordinary use of certain old English words and similar considerations, earlier and better texts of the original had become available, involving many important changes of reading. Thus, while the Translators of 1611 had access only to a few late Greek manuscripts of no special authority, at least two manuscripts of the highest importance, belonging to the fourth century, were now available—the Codex Vaticanus and the Codex Sinaiticus. The knowledge of the versions of the Early Church had also greatly increased, and vastly better aids in the matter of lexicons and grammars had placed scholars in a much more favourable position than any of their predecessors for removing the inaccuracies that had crept into previous translations.

Origin of the Revised Version.

The result was that in May, 1870, the Convocation of the Province of Canterbury decided to ' nominate a body of its own members to undertake the work of revision, who shall be at liberty to invite the co-operation of any eminent for scholarship, to whatever nation or religious body they may belong.'

The Work of Revision.

In terms of this resolution, two Companies were formed for the revision of the Old and of the New Testaments respectively. The New Testament Company consisted at first of twenty-seven, but for the greater part of the time of twenty-four, members and was presided over by Dr. Ellicott, Bishop of Gloucester and Bristol. The Scottish Representatives were : Bishop Wordsworth, St. Andrews ; Principal Brown, F.C. College, Aberdeen ; Professor Eadie, U.P. College, Glasgow ; Professor Milligan, The University, Aberdeen ; and Professor Roberts, The University, St. Andrews. From an early date steps were also taken to secure the valuable aid of American scholars, to whose ' care, vigilance, and accuracy ' the Revisers bear ample testimony in the Preface.[1]

[1] After the time of co-operation with the English Revisers had come to an end, certain survivors of the American Committee in 1901 combined to issue what has come to be known as the Standard American Edition of the Revised Version.

Eight Principles and Rules were laid down for the Revisers' guidance, of which the first five, in view of their importance, may be cited in full :

1. To introduce as few alterations as possible into the Text of the Authorised Version consistently with faithfulness.

2. To limit, as far as possible, the expression of such alterations to the language of the Authorised and earlier English Versions.

3. Each Company to go twice over the portion to be revised, once provisionally, the second time finally, and on principles of voting as hereinafter is provided.

4. That the Text to be adopted be that for which the evidence is decidedly preponderating ; and that when the Text so adopted differs from that from which the Authorised Version was made, the alteration be indicated in the margin.

5. To make or retain no change in the Text on the second final revision by each Company, except *two-thirds* of those present approve of the same, but on the first revision to decide by simple majorities.

The place of meeting of the New Testament Company was the Jerusalem Chamber attached to the Deanery of Westminster Abbey, and already famous as the scene of the preparation of the Westminster Confession of Faith and of the Longer and Shorter Catechisms. The procedure followed was much the same as in the case of the Authorised Version, and was continued over a period of ten and a half years, until at length in 1881 the Revised New Testament was published with the simple title :

The New Testament of our Lord and Saviour, Jesus Christ, translated out of the Greek : being the version set forth A.D. 1611 compared with the most ancient authorities and revised A.D. 1881.

The Value of the Revised Version.

The appearance of the new version aroused the deepest interest both in this country and in the United States, but this is not to say that it was not subjected to much severe criticism, as had been the case with its predecessor. The Revisers' English in particular was strongly attacked, and it was felt that they had sacrificed too much of the old and familiar cadences. This may be the case, and I am not here to defend the Revised Version throughout, but what I do claim is that it gives a more exact and faithful reproduction of the words of the original documents and forms an indispensable companion to the exact study of the New Testament. Take a Parallel New Testament, compare the readings verse by verse and word by word, and you will be amazed at the important changes thus brought to light, necessitated by better authenticated readings and a more accurate understanding of the original Greek.

An obvious example of the latter sort is Acts xxvi. 28, where for the familiar ' Almost thou persuadest me to be a Christian ' we now read ' With but little persuasion thou wouldst fain make me a Christian.' So far from admitting himself to be almost converted, Agrippa rather insinuates that Paul is surely expecting too much from the short conversation that had passed.[1]

Similarly, to turn to another example, when Herodias' daughter danced before Herod and he promised her whatsoever she would ask, ' she,' so we read in our ordinary version, ' being before instructed of her mother, said, Give me here John Baptist's head in a charger ' (Matt. xiv. 8). But the Revised Version, correctly interpreting the Greek verb, has ' she, being put forward by her mother, saith . . , ' clearly indicating that the girl herself was unwilling to make such a proposal, and had to be urged on by her revengeful mother, until at length, as we learn from Mark vi. 25, 'she came in straightway with haste unto the king, and asked, saying, I will that thou forthwith give me in a charger

[1] A similar rendering is found in Purvey's edition of Wyclif : ' And Agrippa saide to Poul, In litil thing thou counseilist me to be maad a Cristen man.'

the head of John the Baptist,' as if it were an errand she would gladly have over as quickly as possible.

Another obvious gain of the Revised Version is the general consistency with which the same Greek word is represented by the same English equivalent. This we know was not the case in the Authorised Version, where the Translators rather prided themselves on the variety of their renderings, and thereby failed to put the modern reader as nearly as possible in the same position as the reader of the original. An example is St. Mark's use of the Greek adverb ($\epsilon\dot{v}\theta\dot{v}s$) for ' straightway,' which occurs no fewer than forty times in his Gospel. Why should this be obscured by the word receiving five different renderings, 'straightway,' ' immediately,' ' forthwith,' ' anon,' and ' as soon as '; while the equally characteristic ' abide ' of St. John's Gospel is rendered indiscriminately ' abide,' ' remain,' ' dwell,' ' continue,' ' tarry,' and ' endure.'

The Doctrinal Significance of the Revised Version.

There remains still the doctrinal significance of the Revised Version which cannot be ignored. For while it is true that it leaves the sum of

Christian doctrine untouched, that is not to say that no new light is thrown upon many truths by the more exact renderings of the later version.

The point is treated with considerable fulness in the present writer's small book on *The Expository Value of the Revised Version*, but a single illustration of what is meant may be cited from it.

Take the great christological passage, Phil. ii. 5-8, and note how ' starting with the thought of Christ's Divinity, the Apostle proceeds to tell us how He Who was thus originally in the form of God counted not this equality of being with God " a prize," a thing to be grasped at or retained, as compared with what by sacrifice He might effect for our sakes, but " emptied Himself," this great act involving, rather than followed by (as the Authorised Version suggests), the two great steps, " taking the form of a servant (bond-servant)," and " being made (becoming) in the likeness of men," while these in turn led to the lowest step of all, " the death of the Cross." How clearly as we note the changes, and more particularly that one bold expression " emptied Himself," so different from the paraphrastic " made Himself of no reputation," is the tremendous reality of our Lord's humiliation brought home to us. And in the verses that follow what new dignity is

added to the exaltation by " the (not " a ")
name which is above every name," which God
gives to Jesus, " in (not " at ") which every
knee should bow." ' [1]

Nothing would be easier than to go on
multiplying examples, but I trust that enough
has been said to prove that the Revised Version
furnishes an aid which no one who desires to
get at the exact meaning of the original Scripture can afford to ignore.   The more it is
studied the more will its so-called blemishes
disappear and every page be found to throw
new and striking light on the inexhaustible
depth of meaning hidden in the Sacred Word.[2]

Fresh Efforts at Revision.

Half a century has passed since the Revised
Version was published, and no attempt on the
same scale has been made to supersede it.   But,
again, there have been a number of what we

[1] It is curious that the Authorised rendering ' at the name
of Jesus,' should first be found in the Genevan Testament
of 1557, and that consequently this version should have
been the means of establishing one of those outward
ceremonies against which the Genevan Reformers set
themselves so strongly.

[2] No better guide for this purpose could be found than
Bishop Westcott's *Some Lessons of the Revised Version of
the New Testament* (London : Hodder & Stoughton, 1897).

may call private attempts in which individual scholars have supplied us with translations, embodying what seemed to them the most important results of recent criticism of the Greek text, and making use of what may be called everyday English, as compared with the more antiquated language of the great Versions.[1]

An early example is offered by the *Twentieth Century New Testament* (1898), the story of whose production is one of the romances of translation. The version sprang, we are told, from the chance remark of a yeoman farmer to a lady visitor at Keswick. ' Why,' he asked, ' is not the Bible written so that we can understand it ? ' And on being told that it was three hundred years since the Authorised Version was published, and that consequently it contained many old words, he not unnaturally put the further question, ' Then why does not some one translate it into English again ? ' The idea took root. The lady made a beginning with a rendering into simple modern English of the first two chapters of St. Mark's Gospel. This came into the hands of a busy engineer. A

[1] Selden in his *Table-Talk* speaks of the *English* Translation of the Bible as ' the best Translation in the World,' but adds in a footnote that ' there is no book so translated, *i.e.* so peculiarly translated, considering the purpose it was meant for—General reading.'

partnership was formed : other workers were enlisted : and arrangements were made for the discussion of such crucial words as Baptism, Church, Gehenna, and so forth. From the beginning the names of the Revisers were with-held from the public, but they included repre-sentatives of different Churches and Univer-sities. No reward was sought save the perfection of the work itself. And it was as ' a labour of love ' that the Translators commended it ' to the good-will of all English-speaking people, and to the blessing of Almighty God.'

About the same time Dr. Weymouth issued his *New Testament in Modern Speech* (1903), in which, following the readings of his *Resultant Greek Testament*, he aimed at furnishing ' a succinct and compressed running commentary (not doctrinal) to be used side by side with its elder compeers.' The version found wide acceptance and passed through various editions, the last in 1929 being enriched with numerous additional illustrative notes at the hands of Professor J. A. Robertson of Aberdeen.

Dr. Moffatt's *The New Testament : A New Translation* (1913 and many later dates) is too well known to require any introduction or description. Its general usefulness has been cordially recognized, nor can there be any question as to the light which it throws upon some of the more difficult passages in the Pauline Epistles. Any criticism that suggests itself is rather in the direction of an occasional use of over-colloquial words and phrases and a tendency to paraphrase rather than to translate.

Along with Dr. Moffatt's may be mentioned a new American translation, which we owe to Professor E. J. Goodspeed of Chicago. Professor Goodspeed is a distinguished papyrologist, and knows how to make the best use of the most recent light thrown upon our New Testament vocabulary. And it is an interesting sign of the times that his translation should have awakened such interest in America, as to have been reprinted in various magazines and newspapers. It is certainly well worth study, and fulfils the translator's aim of bringing home ' the great, living messages of the New Testament a little more widely and forcibly to the life of our time.'

Is Further Revision Necessary ?

But the question remains. Has the time come for a thorough-going revision of our existing translations, a revision in which the best scholarship of the day will be represented, and which will command the confidence of the Church at large ? The question has been raised in various quarters, and interesting experiments have been made of the kind of translation desired. But, on the whole, the general opinion of scholars appears to be that the time for a further authoritative revision is not yet. Many textual problems still await solution before we can hope to have the New Testament autographs in their original form. The vocabulary and grammar of the Greek New Testament are at present the subject of extensive investigation, resulting often in new and fresh meanings being attached to familiar words and phrases. And it must be kept in view that the difficulties of translation, always great, are specially so in the case of our New Testament, where we are met with the demand for a version which, while retaining the dignity and simplicity of the Authorised Version, is at the same time more faithful to the original Greek than it was always possible for that Version to be.

Here, then, we must leave our enquiry. In the present limits it has only been possible to touch upon many of the points raised, but enough, I trust, has been said to bring home the real and living character of our New Testament writings. And, though the exact wording of particular sayings or incidents may still be uncertain, we have the assurance that the main teaching of our Lord rests upon a firm and certain basis.

Meanwhile, the story we have been following is its own best lesson, but if we are to point the moral, it cannot be done better than in the words of the noble Preface to the Authorised Version :

But now, what piety without truth ; what truth, what saving truth, without the word of God. What word of God, whereof we may be sure, without the Scripture. The Scripture we are commanded to search. . . . If we be ignorant they will instruct us ; if out of the way, they will bring us home ; if out of order, they will reform us ; if in heaviness, comfort us ; if dull, quicken us ; if cold, inflame us. *Tolle, lege ; tolle, lege ;* take up and read, take up and read.

APPENDIXES

GLOSSARY

A short list of some of the more technical terms employed

Apparatus criticus : a collection of variant readings (*see under* Variants), generally inserted at the foot of the page containing the text.

Autographs : the original writings of the New Testament.

Bilingual : written in two languages, such as Greek and Latin, the Greek in one column and the Latin in the other.

Citations. *See under* Quotations.

Codex : denotes (1) trunk of a tree ; (2) wooden tablets smeared over with wax and used for ordinary writing purposes ; and (3) any collection of papyrus or parchment sheets laid over one another as in a modern book. *See* p. 15 f.

Conjecture : proposed emendation of what appears to be a corrupt or unintelligible reading. *See* p. 91 f.

Cursive. *See under* Uncial.

Dittography : wrong repetition of a word or syllable.

Families of Manuscripts : collections of documents claiming descent from a common ancestor.

Fathers : applied to Christian writers of the first five centuries.

Gloss : marginal or other addition which has found its way into the text by way of explanation or interpretation.

Haplography : writing a word or syllable once when it should have been written twice.

Homoioteleuton : omission of a verse or line due to the similar ending of adjoining words. *See* p. 19 f.

Lacuna : is used to denote a hole or gap in a papyrus text leading to the loss of a letter, or letters, and consequently making the exact reading uncertain. *See* for example the *lacunae* in Plate II.

Lectionaries : service books containing extracts from the Gospels and Epistles.

Manuscript : a document written by hand.

Majuscule and Minuscule. *See under* Uncial.

Palaeography : the study of ancient handwriting in all its forms.

Palimpsest : lit. ' wrìttēn over again.' *See* p. 17.

Papyrus : writing material prepared from the pith of the stem of the papyrus reed-plant. *See* p. 5 ff.

Parchment : writing material prepared from the skins of sheep and other animals. The name vellum, which was at first applied to a fine variety manufactured from the skins of very young calves, is now practically synonymous. *See* p. 16 f.

Polyglott : a book written in several languages, like the Polyglott Bible edited by Walton containing the New Testament in Greek, Syriac, Latin, Ethiopic and Persian. *See* p. 106 f.

Quotations, Patristic : passages cited from the ' Fathers ' or other early Christian writers.

Recto : the side of a papyrus sheet, on which the fibres lay horizontally, as distinguished from *Verso*, the back of the sheet.

Septuagint : Greek translation of the Hebrew Old Testament.

Textual Criticism : has for its object the removal of errors which have found their way into the text, so as to recover as far as possible the actual words of the original writer.

Textus Receptus : ' the received text,' going back practically to the time of Erasmus, and adopted for long as the traditional Greek text of the Church. It underlies our English Authorised Version.

Type : a class or order of documents distinguished by a particular character. Critics now recognize four types of Greek manuscripts of the New Testament, classifying them under the first four letters of the Greek alphabet—the α-text ; the β-text ; the γ-text ; the δ-text. *See* for example Kenyon, *Handbook*, p. 297 ff.

Uncial (or Majuscule) : *See* p. 29.

Variants, or various readings, arise ' when two or more manuscripts of the same work present different texts in any particular passage.'

Vellum. *See* Parchment.

Versions : translations of the New Testament into the languages of early Christendom, to be carefully distinguished from manuscripts or copies in the original tongue.

Verso. See *Recto*.

Vulgate : usually applied to Jerome's revision of the old Latin text as being the version in ' common ' use.

A BRIEF LIST OF BOOKS FOR ENGLISH
READERS

IN OUR present limits it is impossible to attempt anything in the nature of a bibliography, but a few books
dealing directly with our subject may be mentioned.

Thus, for those who know Greek, Professor Souter's
edition of the Greek New Testament (Oxford : University
Press) based on the text of the Revisers of 1881, with a list
of variant readings, will be found very useful. For students
of the English Revised Version, the edition containing
' fuller references ' (Cambridge : University Press) may
be specially recommended.

Certain external features of our New Testament con-
sidered in Lecture I may be supplemented from F. G.
Kenyon's *Textual Criticism of the New Testament* (London :
Macmillan), p. 19 ff., from the present writer's *New Testament Documents* (London : Macmillan), 1913, and *Here
and There Among the Papyri* (London : Hodder & Stoughton), 1923—both out of print—and from two Essays in
Christianity in the Light of Modern Knowledge (London :
Blackie) dealing with ' The Rise, Language, and Form of
the New Testament Writings ' and ' The Greek Papyri and
the New Testament.'

In the matter of Introduction, Dr. Kirsopp Lake's
Oxford Church Text Book on *The Text of the New Testament*, sixth edition, revised by Silva New (London : Riving-
tons), is a most valuable introduction to the subject, but it
is so compressed that it is not an easy book for the ordinary student.

Of a more popular character are Dr. James Drummond's
Transmission of the Text of the New Testament (London :
The Sunday School Association, 1909), and Dr. Paterson

Smyth's *How We Got Our Bible* (London : Bagster), which has been so widely read.

The fourth edition of Scrivener's indispensable *Introduction to the Criticism of the New Testament* (London : Bell & Sons), edited by the Rev. Edward Miller, contains a full description of the Greek Manuscripts and Ancient Versions. With it may be classed F. G. Kenyon's *Textual Criticism* (as above), and his volume on *Our Bible and the Ancient Manuscripts* (London : Eyre & Spottiswoode), both written in a specially clear and attractive manner. And the same may be said of Professor Souter's *Text and Canon of the New Testament* (London : Duckworth & Co.).

Other books dealing with the subject are Nestle's *Introduction to the Textual Criticism of the Greek New Testament*, English translation by W. Eadie, in Williams and Norgate's Theological Translation Library (London, 1901) ; C. R. Gregory's *Canon and Text of the New Testament* in the International Theological Library (Edinburgh : T. & T. Clark), and A. T. Robertson's *Introduction to the Textual Criticism of the New Testament* (London : Hodder & Stoughton). *See* also *A History of the Textual Criticism of the New Testament* by M. R. Vincent (New York : The Macmillan Company, 1899).

For the history of our English Versions it must be sufficient to refer to such standard works as *The English Bible*, 2 vols., by John Eadie (London : Macmillan) ; *A General View of the History of the English Bible* by B. F. Westcott— third edition revised by W. A. Wright—(London : Macmillan) ; *The History of the English Bible* by W. F. Moulton —fifth edition revised and enlarged—(London : C. H. Kelly).

For further reference the following will be found useful : *The Authorized Edition of the English Bible* (1611), by F. H. A. Scrivener (Cambridge : University Press) ; *Records of the English Bible*, edited by A. W. Pollard (Oxford : University Press), and the same writer's *The Beginning of the New Testament translated by Wm. Tyndale*, 1525 (Oxford : University Press).

The six most important English Translations of the New Testament will be found in *The English Hexapla* preceded by *An Historical Introduction* (London : Bagster) ; and reference may also be made to P. Schaff's *Companion to the Greek Testament and the English Version* (London : Macmillan).

The history of the Revised Version is told by Bishop Ellicott, Chairman of the Revision Committee, in *Addresses on the Revised Version of Holy Scripture* (London : S.P.C.K.), and by S. Newth in *Lectures on Bible Revision* (London : Hodder & Stoughton).

For a general summary I may be permitted to refer to my Guild Text Book, *The English Bible : A Sketch of its History* (London : A. & C. Black), and to *The Expository Value of the Revised Version* (Edinburgh : T. & T. Clark).

APPENDIX OF ADDITIONAL NOTES

NOTE A

GREEK PAPYRUS LETTERS

As FURTHER illustrating the epistolary form of New Testament times, the following letter is of interest, in which a soldier, Apion, who had been despatched to Italy, writes to his father to announce his safe arrival. The letter belongs to the second century, and the original is edited in the *Berliner Griechische Urkunden*, ii, No. 423 (=Milligan, *Selections from the Greek Papyri*, p. 90 ff.).

Apion to Epimachus his father and lord heartiest greetings. First of all I pray that you are in health and continually prosper and fare well with my sister and her daughter and my brother. I thank the lord Serapis that when I was in danger at sea he saved me. Straightway when I entered Misenum I received my travelling money from Caesar, three gold pieces. And I am well. I beg you therefore, my lord father, write me a few lines, first regarding your health, secondly regarding that of my brother and sister, thirdly that I may kiss your hand, because you have brought me up well, and on this account I hope to be quickly promoted, if the gods will. Give many greetings to Capito, and to my brother and sister, and to Serenilla, and my friends. I send you a little portrait of myself at the hands of Euctemon. And my (military) name is Antoni(u)s Maximus. I pray for your good health.

Company Athenonike.

Serenus the son of Agathos Daemon greets you . . . and Turbo the son of Gallonius and . . .

(Addressed)

To Philadelphia for Epimachus from his son Apion.

Then the following addition :

Give this to the (office of the) first cohort of the Apamaeans to Julianus . . . paymaster from Apion, so that (he may forward it) to Epimachus his father.

With this letter may be compared a letter addressed by a mother to her children in the second or the beginning of the third century. The original is edited in the *Berliner Griechische Urkunden*, i, No. 332 (= Milligan, *Thessalonians*, p. 128).

Serapias to her children Ptolemaeus and Apolinaria and Ptolemaeus heartiest greeting. Above all I pray that you may be in health, which is for me the most necessary of all things. I make my obeisance to the lord Serapis, praying that I may receive word that you are in health, even as I pray for your general welfare. I rejoiced when I received letters that you were well recovered. Salute Ammonous with his children and wife and those who love you. Cyrilla saluteth you, and Hermias the daughter of Hermias, Hermanoubis the nurse, Athenais the teacher (?), Cyrilla, Casia . . . Empis, in fact all who are here. Please therefore write me what you are about, for you know that, if I receive your letters, I am glad on account of your well-being. I pray that you may prosper.

On the *Verso* the letter has two addresses, one in the original hand to the effect :

Deliver to Ptolemaeus my child. Salute . . .

And the second in a different hand :

Deliver to Ptolemaeus the brother of Apolinaria.

Note B

RECENT ARCHAEOLOGICAL DISCOVERIES

In the course of the present enquiry we have had to make frequent reference to recent archaeological discoveries in their bearing on the New Testament, as, for example, in the cases of the Sinaitic and Washington Codices among Greek Manuscripts, and the Old Syriac and Lewis Gospels among Early Versions. And now, as this book is being prepared for the press, widespread interest has once more been aroused by the discovery of new Biblical papyri from Egypt. They form part of the Chester Beatty Collection, and their publication has been entrusted to the well-known papyrologist and textual critic, Sir Frederic Kenyon. Some time must necessarily elapse before the documents can be thoroughly examined, but meanwhile Sir Frederic Kenyon has given a summary description in *The Times* for 19th November, 1931, from which we may gather a few particulars.

The exact place of origin of the papyri is unknown, but there can be little doubt that they have come from the Library of a Christian Church or Monastery in Egypt. In themselves they consist of one hundred and ninety papyrus leaves, many very fragmentary but amazingly legible considering their age. Nine contain parts of different books of the Old Testament, and to them may be added a considerable portion of the Greek text of the apocryphal book of Enoch. As regards the New Testament, with which we are specially concerned, one papyrus codex, when complete, must have contained the Four Gospels and Acts, while another huge codex seems to have included all the Pauline Epistles with the exception of the Pastorals. By the courtesy of *The Times*, we are able to show as a frontispiece two leaves of this latter codex.

The age of the papyri is even more remarkable than their extent. The larger number belong to the third century, but according to Sir Frederic Kenyon and other competent critics, the earliest can be assigned with confidence to an early date in the second century. They are thus amongst the oldest manuscripts as yet known of the Greek Bible, and students will await eagerly the results of their further examination and collation at the hands of experts.

Note C

ADDITIONAL UNCIAL MANUSCRIPTS

It may be of interest to add one or two furthe examples of our uncial manuscripts in view of certain special characteristics which they possess :

Codex Laudianus : So named because once in the possession of Archbishop Laud who presented it to the Bodleian Library in 1636. A Latin-Greek manuscript with Latin in the place of honour on the left, pointing to a comparatively late date, probably the first half of the seventh century. The writing is in thick rude uncials, and the Latin has been made to correspond closely with the Greek. Its main interest for us, however, is that it was used by the Venerable Bede, who quotes from it in his *Expositio* and *Liber*

Retractationis. It was, accordingly, one of the first Greek manuscripts to be used in such a way.

Codex Regius : An eighth century manuscript of the four Gospels, which has many close points of contact with the text of the Vatican Codex, though it has been badly written and contains many ignorant blunders. It has, however, the special interest that it contains two endings of St. Mark's Gospel : the longer ending as it appears in our canonical Mark, and a shorter ending following ch. xvi. 9 which runs as follows :

And all that had been commanded them they briefly reported to Peter and those who were with him and after this Jesus himself appeared to them, and from the East and as far as to the West sent forth through them the sacred and incorruptible proclamation of eternal salvation.

Codex Augiensis : A ninth century Graeco-Latin manuscript of the Pauline Epistles, which belonged to the English scholar Bentley (cf. p. 108), and on his death passed into the possession of Trinity College, Cambridge. The writing of the Greek is in neat square uncials, but some of the pages are disfigured by Latin notes scrawled in the margins. The Epistle to the Hebrews is given only in Latin.

Codex Rossanensis : Belonging to the sixth century and written with silver letters on purple vellum, while the first three lines of each gospel are in gold as also the names of ' God ' and ' Jesus.' It is one of the oldest known manuscripts illustrated with miniatures.

Codex W^d : May be mentioned, if only as recalling the strange sources from which some of our manuscripts have been recovered. When the Librarian of Trinity College, Cambridge, was engaged in binding a copy of Gregory Nazianzen he picked out from the packing in the back of the book some twenty-seven different fragments of ancient Greek writing. On examination these proved to have been part of a manuscript of St. Mark belonging to the ninth century. The text as a rule is very similar to the text of the great uncials, but one reading appears to be unique. In Mark vii. 33 the words run : ' He [Jesus] spat upon his fingers, and put them into the ears of the deaf man, and He touched the tongue of the man of thick speech.' See further Rendel Harris, *The Diatessaron of Tatian*, Appendix, p. 62 ff. (Cambridge University Press, 1890).

NOTE D

THE ABGARUS LETTERS

EUSEBIUS HAS preserved for us the text of the Abgarus Letters in his *Church History*, i, 13. The translation is by the Rev. A. C. McGiffert in *The Library of Nicene and Post-Nicene Fathers*, New Series, vol. i.

Copy of an epistle written by Abgarus the ruler to Jesus, and sent to him at Jerusalem by Ananias the swift courier.

Abgarus, ruler of Edessa, to Jesus the excellent Saviour who has appeared in the country of Jerusalem, greeting. I have heard the reports of thee and of thy cures as performed by thee without medicines or herbs. For it is said that thou makest the blind to see and the lame to walk, that thou cleansest lepers and castest out impure spirits and demons, and that thou healest those afflicted with lingering disease, and raisest the dead. And having heard all these things concerning thee, I have concluded that one of two things must be true : either thou art God, and having come down from heaven thou doest these things, or else thou, who doest these things, art the Son of God. I have therefore written to thee to ask thee that thou wouldest take the trouble to come to me and heal the disease which I have. For I have heard that the Jews are murmuring against thee and are plotting to injure thee. But I have a very small yet noble city which is great enough for us both.

The answer of Jesus to the ruler Abgarus by the courier Ananias.

Blessed art thou who hast believed in me without having seen me. For it is written concerning me, that they who have seen me will not believe in me, and that they who have not seen me will believe and be saved. But in regard to what thou hast written me, that I should come to thee, it is necessary for me to fulfil all things here for which I have been sent, and after I have fulfilled them thus to be taken up again to him that sent me. But after I have been taken up I will send to thee one of my disciples, that he may heal thy disease and give life to thee and thine.

See also F. C. Burkitt, *Early Eastern Christianity* (London : Murray, 1904), p. 10 ff.

NOTE E

THE VERSE-DIVISIONS IN THE NEW TESTAMENT

AN EARLIER division into verses than that contained in Stephanus' Greek Testament of 1551 had appeared in Pagninus' Latin translation of the New Testament from Hebrew and Greek published at Lyons in 1527-28. For further particulars regarding these verse-divisions, see Ezra Abbot, *Critical Essays*, p. 464 ff., on ' The Division of the Greek New Testament into

Verses,' being the first part of the *Prolegomena* to Tischendorf's eighth edition.

The dangers attending verse-divisions are strongly put by John Locke in his *Essay for the Understanding of St. Paul's Epistles* (London, 1823), where (Preface, p. 7 f.) he shows that by the dividing of them into chapters and verses the Epistles ' are so chopped and minced, and, as they are now printed, stand so broken and divided, that not only the common people take the verses usually for distinct aphorisms ; but even men of more advanced knowledge, in reading them, lose very much of the strength and force of the coherence and the light that depends on it. . . . When the eye is constantly disturbed in loose sentences, that by their standing and separation appear as so many distinct fragments ; the mind will have much ado to take in, and carry on in its memory, an uniform discourse of dependent reasonings ; . . . These divisions also have given occasion to the reading these epistles by parcels, and in scraps, which has farther confirmed the evil arising from such partitions. And I doubt not but every one will confess it to be a very unlikely way, to come to the understanding of any other letters, to read them piece-meal, a bit to-day, and another scrap to-morrow, and so on by broken intervals ; especially if the pause and cessation should be made, as the chapters the apostle's epistles are divided into, do end sometimes in the middle of a discourse, and sometimes in the middle of a sentence. It cannot therefore but be wondered that that should be permitted to be done to holy writ, which would visibly disturb the sense, and hinder the understanding of any other book whatsoever.'

The division into chapters which we still use goes back to the twelfth century, and was the work of Stephen Langton, afterwards Archbishop of Canterbury.

NOTE F

EXTRACTS FROM THE TRANSLATORS' PREFACE TO THE AUTHORISED VERSION, 1611

THE TRANSLATORS' Preface to the Authorised Version of 1611 is a lengthy but exceedingly interesting document, generally understood to be the work of Dr. Miles Smith, afterwards Bishop of Gloucester. It no longer appears in our modern editions of the Bible, doubtless owing to its length, but single copies can be easily procured through the Bible Agencies. To do it justice the Preface must be studied in its entirety, but a few brief extracts will show the manner and spirit in which the work of translation was carried through. The spelling has been modernized.

After some introductory remarks on the calumnies which follow all reformers and revisers, the translators pass to a beautiful eulogy in praise of the Holy Scriptures. ' And what marvel ? ' they ask. ' The original thereof being from heaven, not from earth : the author being God, not man : the inditer, the Holy Spirit, not the wit of the Apostles or Prophets : the penmen, such as were sanctified from the womb, and endued with a principal portion of God's Spirit : . . . Happy is the man that delighteth in the Scripture, and thrice happy that meditateth in it day and night.'

'But how,' they continue, 'shall men meditate in that which they cannot understand ? How shall they understand that which is kept close in an unknown tongue ? . . . Translation it is that openeth the window, to let in the light : that breaketh the shell, that we may eat the kernel : that putteth aside the curtain, that we may look into the most Holy place.'

A long account of previous translations follows, and the labours of English workers in this field are held to be deserving of 'everlasting remembrance.' 'Yet for all that,' they say, ' as nothing is begun and perfected at the same time, and the latter thoughts are thought to be the wiser : so, if we building upon their foundation that went before us, and being holpen by their labours, do endeavour to make that better which they left so good, no man, we are sure, hath cause to mislike us ; they, we persuade ourselves, if they were alive, would thank us.' Certain cavils of their adversaries are then met, and after again alluding to their own purpose in translating, the translators conclude : ' It remaineth, that we commend thee (gentle Reader) to God, and to the Spirit of his grace, which is able to build further than we can ask or think. He removeth the scales from our eyes, the vail from our hearts, opening our wits, that we may understand his word, enlarging our hearts, yea, correcting our affections, that we may love it above gold and silver, yea, that we may love it to the end. . . . Others have laboured, and you may enter into their labours ; O receive not so great things in vain : O despise not so great salvation ! . . . It is a fearful thing to fall into the hands of the living God ; but a blessed thing it is, and will bring us to everlasting blessedness in the end, when God speaketh unto us, to hearken ; when he setteth his word before us, to read it ; when he stretcheth out his hand and calleth, to answer, Here am I, here we are to do thy will, O God. The Lord work a care and conscience in us to know him and serve him, that we may be acknowledged of him at the appearing of our Lord JESUS CHRIST, to whom with the Holy Ghost be all praise and thanksgiving. Amen.'

I. AUTHORS AND SUBJECTS

[For the principal Subjects dealt with, reference should be made to the Table of Contents and to the Glossary.]

201

II. NEW TESTAMENT REFERENCES

PRINTED IN GREAT BRITAIN BY ROBERT MACLEHOSE AND CO. LTD.
THE UNIVERSITY PRESS GLASGOW